HAPPY & SECURE IN SONOMA COUNTY

PIECING TOGETHER THE PUZZLE OF FINANCIAL SECURITY AND HAPPINESS IN THIS CHOSEN SPOT OF ALL THE EARTH

BY

MONTGOMERY TAYLOR

PRAISE FOR *HAPPY & SECURE IN SONOMA COUNTY*

"Montgomery Taylor has offered up a diverse set of localized resources woven together through a series of personal stories. It is a pleasurable read with a generous helping of advice towards a more secure life."

— Doug Hilberman
President, AXIA Architects

"As a pastor in Sonoma County, I was very interested in the premise of Monty's new book. How to be happy in this beautiful place is a question with rich religious overtones. While this book is not theological, its sage advice can certainly be used that way. From the Bible's perspective, wealth is primarily a means of blessing others. Thankfully, this book has some of these kinds of stories. If you are interested in gaining wealth to convert to the highest purpose now or after you are gone, prudence dictates a strategy. Monty has plenty of good advice to help reach the goal."

— V. Mark Smith
Pastor, Berean Baptist Church

"Happy & Secure in Sonoma County is a thoroughly enjoyable read. Its personal stories demonstrate the diversity of life in Sonoma County and the associated financial challenges we all face. The case-study approach provides practical guidance, and usable financial tips that can be easily understood and put into practice. Montgomery Taylor's holistic approach to wealth management, as illustrated through this book, is a breath of fresh air...Sonoma County air."

— Áine Smalley
Senior Regulatory Affairs Director, Medtronic

"Montgomery Taylor has written a detailed, informative book which addresses issues that matter to all of us who live, work and plan to retire in Sonoma County. You need not be a financial expert to grasp the concepts and advice provided. I recommend this book to anyone seeking useful advice on how to be financially secure, regardless of your situation."

— Pete Foppiano
Broker, Golden Bear Financial, former Healdsburg Mayor

"Happy & Secure in Sonoma County *gives every individual advice for a sustainable retirement. The readable format of case scenarios allows the readers to imagine being in that person's shoes. Monty creates and implements a step-by-step financial plan that is achievable. Expert advice from insurance, legal, healthcare, and real estate professionals complete the package. An achievable plan ultimately affects our wellbeing, peace of mind and happiness."*

— Barbara Cooper
Registered Nurse (Retired), Kaiser Permanente

"Timely and easy to read, Happy & Secure in Sonoma County *offers insightful information without being complicated. It inspires one to take action and realistic steps toward being better prepared for future retirement. A great resource!"*

— Kris Wilson
Development Director, Santa Rosa Memorial Hospital Foundation

"My favorite part of this book is how it includes detailed, personal stories that illustrate the human side of financial planning, then uses those words to provide a framework for helpful feedback and tools that readers can use to better plan their future. It has solid advice that covers situations that many of us might not think about—but should."

— Julie Fadda Powers
Editor, *NorthBay biz* magazine

"Warren Buffet said, 'You don't have to be a genius to invest well.' He's right and the way to do it is through a multi-pronged approach to investing with the help of quality professionals. Montgomery Taylor's new book, Happy & Secure in Sonoma County, *lays out real life stories and strategies that bring peace of mind and a secure retirement future."*

— Joe Brogan
Senior Vice President (Retired), Unimac Corp.

— Alanna Brogan
Professor, Sonoma State University

"No theory. No jargon. No doubletalk. Just good practical advice about building financial security and enjoying the financial freedom to be happy. Happy & Secure in Sonoma County *is a great roadmap for success that reminds us we are all in control of our destiny, and the choices we make and the priorities we establish will have long term and lasting impacts on our lives. The real life client stories, the advisor's perspective and the sections on making it happen; all add up to an entertaining and compelling read. Monty lays out a complete plan which should dramatically help people improve their lives."*

— Michael Downey
Senior Vice President / Business Services, Redwood Credit Union

"We all strive to achieve financial independence and security enabling us to live life to the fullest. Here is a practical, easy-to-read book that is helpful in realizing these goals."

— Connie Codding
President, Codding Foundation

"From baby boomer to grandparent, this book will ultimately affect us all. Happy & Secure in Sonoma County *is a practical and smart guide to mastering your relationship with money."*

— Kirk Veale
Owner, Veale Outdoor Advertising

"A topic way too neglected by many, although so vital to one's enjoyability of their retirement years. This is a must read, to get the earliest possible handle on a critically important part of life. Monty's book even has a great action plan with many of the tools needed for guiding one through the process of planning for financial security. And I loved being so well informed through several relatable real life stories!"

— Larry Dahl
President & CEO, Oilstop Inc.

"Happy & Secure in Sonoma County *is an effective method of learning and gaining financial knowledge by reading other people's real life scenarios. It feels more relevant knowing their stories come from Sonoma County where my own financial planning will largely take place as well. That makes the book that much more interesting and fun."*

— Sam Tamayo
Vice Chairman & Chief Innovation Officer, La Tortilla Factory

For a larger collection of client and student comments about Montgomery Taylor's work as well as information about his other books, newsletters, and services, visit these websites:

www.taxwiseadvisor.com

www.ciorep.com

www.calethics.org

http://montgomerytaylor.thenewrulesofsuccess.com

www.happyandsecureinsonomacounty.com

HAPPY & SECURE IN SONOMA COUNTY

PIECING TOGETHER THE PUZZLE OF FINANCIAL SECURITY AND HAPPINESS IN THIS CHOSEN SPOT OF ALL THE EARTH

BY

MONTGOMERY TAYLOR

WITH SPECIAL GUEST CONTRIBUTORS:

Mortgage Consultant, Rich Abazia
Home Care Consultant, Lucy Andrews, RN, MS
Family Law Attorney, Jeanne Browne, Esq.
Business Law Attorney, William F. Fritz, Esq.
Estate and Trust Attorney, Eric Gullotta, JD, CPA, MS (Tax)
Philanthropic Consultant, Kay Marquet
Realtor, Susan Pack
Health Insurance Consultant/Broker, Teri Sackett

www.bookstandpublishing.com

Published by
Bookstand Publishing
Morgan Hill, CA 95037
4237_7

ISBN 978-1-63498-056-2

DISCLAIMER

This publication is designed to provide accurate and authoritative information with
regard to the subject matter covered. It is sold with the understanding that the
publisher is not engaged in rendering legal, accounting, or other professional advice.
If legal advice or other expert assistance is required, the services of a competent
professional should be sought. The opinions expressed by the authors in this book
are not endorsed by Bookstand Publishing and are the sole responsibility of the
author rendering the opinion.

This book is available at special quantity discounts for bulk purchases for sales
promotions, premiums, fundraising, and educational use. Special versions or book
excerpts can also be created to fit specific needs.
For more information, please write:
Montgomery Taylor
2880 Cleveland Avenue, Suite 2
Santa Rosa, CA 95403

Or call (707) 576-8700
Visit us online:
www.HappyAndSecureInSonomaCounty.com
www.TaxWiseAdvisor.com

Printed in the United States of America

To my mom and dad, who brought our family to Sonoma County in 1958 and taught me how to be happy and secure.

To my wife, Terri, and our children, Luisa, Shannon, and Joseph.

Contents

FREE OFFERS AND RESOURCES FROM MONTGOMERY TAYLOR

Acknowledgments

The best part of my journey has been the people I've had the good fortune to meet and know. I love going to work every day and spending time with talented and enthusiastic teammates. As anyone who's written a book knows, it takes a lot of time, but with the right team, it's a bit easier. I want to thank everyone who helped me get this book to the shelf.

I cherish the wonderful clients who allowed me to interview them and who agreed to share intimate details of their financial lives. Without their selfless contributions, this book would not have been possible. Its clients such as these that make it such a joy to want to do the best for them.

For their expertise and whose professionalism I highly regard, I'd like to thank Rich Abazia, Lucy Andrews, RN, MS, Jeanne Browne, Esq., William F. Fritz, Esq., Eric Gullotta, JD, CPA, MS (Tax), Kay Marquet, Susan Pack, and Teri Sackett. As co-authors, they each shared in the rigors of the many, many steps it takes to bring a book to completion.

I would like to thank Seth Howland for the many hours of administration work he capably put forth to keep this project on time and on budget. A huge thanks to Natalie Koppen for her writing assistance on the case study stories.

For reading the manuscript in its various stages and their refreshing comments, suggestions and edits, I'm grateful to Pat Lucas, Barbara Shaw and Sandy Koppen. The many hours they put in truly enhanced the readability of this book.

For the book cover, I thank my wife Terri for taking the photograph of the beautiful vineyard and blue sky out near the City of Sonoma. The artistic cover design was created by Brandon Holcombe. Thanks goes to Danielle Putonen for the interior layout and design.

For those who felt this book worthy of their endorsement, our heartfelt thanks.

Preface

Luther Burbank, the renowned horticulturist who made his home in Sonoma County, said, *"...this is the chosen spot of all this earth as far as Nature is concerned."*

Some in my family would say this is the chosen spot of all the earth for hay-fever. Fortunately, that hasn't been my experience. I love Sonoma County. I grew up here and have lived here all my life, except for a short stint living in Washington D.C. working for the FBI.

I am on a mission to get you feeling happy and secure in Sonoma County. And let me tell you, I'm excited about this mission—not only excited to be here in this chosen spot, but to be a husband, a father, an enthusiastic entrepreneur, and working in a vocation where I can help others achieve their financial goals. My greatest hope is that what I put down in these pages may inspire and help you and others by offering an honest look at who I am inside, and what steps I've taken to help others to be happy and secure.

I believe I'm smarter today than I was yesterday, and I know I'm a lot smarter than I was ten, twenty, or thirty years ago. I'm smart enough now to value the experiences I've had over the half-century I've been in this world, and I know that the ones who count are all a result of the choices I've made. But I also know that many people aren't aware that there *are* choices to be made, that they *do* have control over a lot of what happens to them. The freedom to choose the way we live our lives is one of the greatest gifts we've been given, and it's a gift you should open. That's what I hope you'll glean from what I share with you.

Many of us go through life without really thinking about who we are or why we do the things we do. It's as if we're living on autopilot, staring straight ahead without seeing anything other than what's right in front of our faces. I know what this feels like because it's happened to me, and I know how easy it is to become passive. We do things or agree to things or accept whatever comes our way without considering whether or not it's right for us. And by passively accepting whatever happens, we give up chances every day to create the lives we want.

It doesn't have to be that way. You can make choices in your life; in fact, you *must* make choices in order to have the life you want, instead of the one that just happens to you. And whether or not you're aware of it, you *do* make choices all the time; even choosing not to choose is a choice.

I believe we were put on this earth to enjoy lives of joy and abundance, and that is what I want for you and for me. I want to get you excited about whatever phase of life you're in, excited about being in Sonoma County, excited about being happy and secure.

And it's all there for the choosing, because I believe in the core of my being that how you live, how I live, how we all live is largely a matter of choice. We have the right to choose to be happy. We have the right to choose to have a good attitude. It's all a choice.

Abraham Lincoln said, *"Folks are usually about as happy as they make their minds up to be."* I'll add to that—you don't need a lot of costly stuff to be happy. If your "needs" are met, you should feel secure. Security in your life opens up the freedom to relax and be happy.

This book is about making choices for building your financial security and making you happy. The ideas included here can enable you to <u>worry</u> less about your money and <u>enjoy</u> it more. You don't have to adopt all the ideas. Even a few performed consistently can make a big difference in your outlook on life. They have in mine.

Making good choices about money is essential, but just remember . . .

What Money Can't Buy

In the book, *Money and the Meaning of Life: Spiritual Search in a Material World* (Bantam Doubleday Dell, 1991), Jacob Needleman affirms what you've always felt and yet he still manages to surprise you. He asks the question, "What's the one thing money can't buy?" Happiness? Good health? Love? While these answers are true sometimes, they are not universal. Money can buy the experiences that let happiness and even love rise in us. Often, good health is relative to money. For example, if two people have the exact same illness, who do you think is more likely getting the better care? The patient with money. So what is the one thing money can't buy? (Of course, your mind is wandering to the answer given in that country song by Guy Clark, *"True love and homegrown tomatoes."*)

Needleman writes that, universally and throughout time, the one thing money can't buy is meaning. That statement is brilliant, both as an insight and as an opportunity for us.

The opportunity is for us to reevaluate our priorities. I'm hopeful that the material thoughtfully placed within this book will do just that—get you thinking and reevaluating—so that you too can be happy and secure in Sonoma County.

Hopefully, I can persuade you of one other thing. There are those of you who are adamant about "living in the moment." You think that mastering the moment is crucial for living happily and enjoying leisure. You think that getting life insurance, on *your* life at least, is silly because when you're dead, you're dead. You hope you bounce your last check on the day you die. You think that he who dies with the most toys, wins. And you think wise the Scottish proverb, "Be happy while you are alive because you are a long time dead."

I believe living joy-filled days is optimal, but I also believe that a balanced life is important. I've seen the devastation brought upon families of those who live only in the moment, casting to the wind any care or concern for tomorrow. Just keep in mind, for your family's sake, that the sun <u>will</u> rise tomorrow and a roof overhead and food on the table are necessary, whether you're unemployed, disabled, retired or dead.

Don't let the sun go down today without taking at least one step, even a small step, to ensure that all your tomorrows, and your family's tomorrows, will be happy and secure.

Montgomery Taylor
Santa Rosa, 2015

Introduction

From Rags to Riches . . . Is the American Dream Still Alive?

The term "American Dream" was coined in 1931 by J.T. Adams, a U.S. writer and historian. The British Dictionary provides the following definition: "the notion that the American social, economic, and political system makes success possible for every individual." I read someone's personal definition in a Press Democrat article a while back that went like this: "The American Dream is to have your own house with a white picket fence, a dog running around the backyard, and a happy family." Actually, I thought this definition would have been the one in the dictionary. Perhaps I'm naïve or it's just my 'country boy,' who grew up in the 50s and 60s, shining through.

I understand how it may seem like a fading dream to those who have suffered a huge financial setback in recent years. Whether you lost your house or your job—or both—it certainly could be cause for an eroding faith in the good ol' American Dream. I'm happy to say that I'm an optimist. My faith is not wavering—not for a minute. Without faith, you're without hope. 'Hopeless' is a sad and unnecessary place to be. I like to think that each day is a new day—ready for new decisions and outcomes. We just need to smile and decide what we want for ourselves, then put the pieces of that puzzle together.

Personally, my life has taken many different twists and turns. I grew up on a farm with a dad who was so frugal that I would have thought I was dirt poor—if I knew what that meant. The truth is I had everything I needed and more . . . a roof over my head, clothes on my back, food on the table, and a family that loved me. Oh, and some shiny new toys every birthday and Christmas.

I thought about acting as a career, though never pursued it. I tried selling vacuum cleaners, the Marine Corps, law enforcement, and working as a stock broker before I found my direction. The thing is, I always figured I could choose my direction and change it when I wanted to. I never felt shackled to anything.

There have been times when I have been very poor—not an extra nickel to my name. I know what it's like to scrimp and save in order to get to the end of the month before the money runs out. When Terri and I were newlyweds, we lived in an apartment near Snoopy's ice arena in Santa Rosa. We had NO money, so for our date nights we'd walk over to Snoopy's and watch people skate. Sometimes we would even "splurge" and buy a cup of hot cocoa. In one of the first houses we rented in Rohnert Park, the living room sat vacant—for three years—because we couldn't afford any furniture. Perhaps this is why I am so inspired by people like Louisa May Alcott, Gene Kelly, Charlie Chaplin, Amelia Earhart, Harry Morgan, and Jackie Cooper, who all overcame so many challenges and became so successful. I have many role models who inspire me to push onward and upward, fitting together the puzzle pieces of the American Dream.

The truth is America is full of success stories of people pulling themselves up by their bootstraps. Yes, even today. *You may say I'm a dreamer, but I'm not the only one . . .*

Putting the Puzzle Together

Section I of this book has 9 Chapters; the first 7 begin with stories about the lives of specific clients who have agreed to share their experiences—with names changed. These stories of real live people here in Sonoma County will

 You will see this happy little puzzle piece when I introduce a new tool or suggested step for your consideration.

give you food for thought. You can learn from their mistakes and their successes. You may notice that most of them are women: This is simply because women were the ones who stepped forward when I put out a request for candidates willing to share. I follow up each story with an "Advisor's Perspective" section and a "Making it Happen" section. Don't think of the suggested steps provided as being in sequential order, that must be followed 1, 2, and 3. Instead, you might think of these as puzzle pieces laid out on a table, waiting for you to fit them together in a way that works best for you. You can also treat this section as a cafeteria line, choosing whatever steps seem most important to you at the moment. Each chapter also includes a little discussion on an applicable income tax planning topic—just as in my office, tax planning is integrated with all other planning.

Chapters 8 and 9 are intended to stretch your thinking and attitude about creating wealth and a successful retirement lifestyle, as well as keeping your family wealth secure for future generations.

Section II is a collection of eight Bonus Chapters, each written by a different local expert, addressing different aspects of wealth accumulation, wealth preservation and finding happiness and security in Sonoma County. Some of the authors are people I work with or know in different ways, and some are clients of mine. I invited them to contribute, and they were pleased to share their knowledge with you. Their chapters were prepared exclusively for this book.

Section III, Financial Independence Resources, includes a directory of contact information for each co-author expert as well as many of the other individuals mentioned throughout the book, and people you need to meet and books you should read if you are very serious about wealth and financial independence. See the free resources page at the end of the book for a complete listing, including: Net Worth Planning Worksheet in Excel, 57 Point Financial Health Checklist, "Tax Bomb" White Paper, Social Security Optimization Report, Better Retirement Returns Report, and more.

Your happiness and security require that you take control of your destiny. This book will help you do just that.

Although I address many issues of interest to those who are retired or about to retire, let me stress that this is not a retirement book, nor is it simply a financial book. It is a *happiness* book that deals with financial and retirement issues. These issues affect every member of your family, be it you, your spouse, your children or your aging parents. You should share this book with members of your family, since they will be impacted by your decisions.

Share this book with your professional advisors—your attorney, tax advisor, financial planner, and the director of your local office on aging—since these people will be crucial in aiding you.

Each chapter is designed to give you the information and the tools you will need to grow in happiness and security. The way I see it, you will have attained this happiness and security when you can get up in the morning when you want to get up, go to sleep when you want to go to sleep, and work and play at the things you want to work and play at, all at your own pace. The good news is that by reading this book you are on the way to doing just that.

SECTION I

Chapter 1

Money Doesn't Buy Happiness —
Even in Sonoma County

I think money can buy a lot of things, but happiness is not really one of them. Sure, we all need a certain amount of money. Beyond that, I have found happiness in other places.

Patricia's Story

Does money buy happiness? Well, growing up in Redwood Falls, Minnesota, my family was always extremely frugal. My grandmother was known for her thrifty touches like ironing out and reusing gift wrap! My siblings and I worked hard in our father's dry cleaning plant for our allowances, and my Depression-era parents ingrained this guiding bit of wisdom into our heads: "Do you want it, or do you need it?" We also valued education a lot in our family, and throughout high school I just knew that I was going to go to college and become a teacher. However, when I got pregnant in my senior year of high school, my whole life outlook changed. I went from planning to be a career woman to eloping to Sonoma County and preparing to be a family woman. Starting off with $100 from the sale of my saxophone, I babysat and my husband worked in a warehouse. We had to save pennies wherever we could just to live and take care of our son. I started attending College of Marin, spent one year at San Francisco State and eventually attended Sonoma State University full time to pursue my passion for education and teaching; I majored in German and minored in French and English. I taught English, French, German, Spanish and video production at a local high school for 35 years, and I absolutely loved it. After many years, my husband and I divorced and I went back to school. I earned my Master's degree in 1988, which improved my teacher's pay. I still loved teaching and doing all kinds of kooky things with the kids, like coming to class as my alter ego, Fifi LaRouge, or putting together crazy costumes for the annual Bop-Til-You-Drop senior fundraiser. But in 2002, I started to feel more tired than usual, so in 2004 I went to the doctor and found out I had lymphoma. But I survived! A while after my treatment, in 2006, I was asked to come back to the school and substitute teach for a couple more years until 2008.

Now, in retirement, I'm happier than ever. My teacher's pension is pretty good, so I feel like I have plenty of money to live on (and splurge occasionally!) I'm mostly just glad I don't have to work at McDonald's at age 74! My only regret is briefly using my house as a bank/ATM (paying off credit cards with home equity lines of credit), which means that my mortgage won't be paid off until I'm well into my 80s. But I've continued to be thrifty, doing a lot of things, like making rather than buying gifts, to keep myself content financially. I do believe that financial planning is essential for survival in the American economy, and I've had my share of experience with different advisors and such. Most of them just tried to sell me things. The only satisfactory experiences I've had were with advisors who really planned out retirement and the future for me without forcing me to invest all over the place. I want to enjoy retirement now and maybe have money left over, to pass on to my kids when I die (at age 101 and not a day sooner)!

My personal belief is that money doesn't buy happiness past about $75,000. Happiness is being able to go on vacations and do things the family wants to do; it's being able to have a not-so-tight budget and squander your cash every once in a while. Retirement has meant so much to me beyond financial stability. I love volunteering, taking care of my dog, reading two newspapers every morning, drinking my coffee slowly, just taking time with life. I love planning for huge family gatherings and finding vegan recipes the whole family can enjoy. I can really help out with my favorite charity, the American Cancer Society, which helped me get the miracle drug I needed when I had cancer. I've also become really passionate about photography, scrapbooking and genealogy. I love to work for hours on family trees and figuring out our family history; I hope that future generations will value my work and maybe even put it in a museum! My passion for education can also run wild, and I love going to the local Osher Lifelong Learning Institute at Sonoma State University. Above all else, my main goal in retirement is to be the ultimate grandma and be there for all my grandkids' and great-grandkids' milestones and birthdays.

The area I've settled in is also a huge factor in my happiness in retirement. Luther Burbank was right when he said that Sonoma County was the "chosen spot of all this earth as far as Nature is concerned!" Everything grows here, and we have the Green Music Center and so many other wonderful places to go. We have great values, too—we love to recycle, we're locavores, we love healthy fast food, and we have access to great health care. I have to stay here to keep my health insurance from my job, but I'm glad to do it. I have quite a few friends who've moved to Arizona or Nevada or Alaska and they regret it because it's so hard to afford to buy back into this area if you leave. Overall, I'd have to say that retirement has left me happy and secure in Sonoma County.

The Advisor's Perspective

After her prior advisor passed away, Patricia was referred to me by another one of my clients. Initially, she needed help with income tax preparation, which we took care of. Shortly thereafter, I met with her regarding her investments and financial planning. As a retired teacher, Patricia had a nice pension check coming every month from CalSTRS, the California State Teachers' Retirement System. In addition to that, she owned a house and had accumulated $260,000 in an IRA.

I found Patricia to be a very sweet, good natured person. She is always smiling and light-hearted in her ways. With all that she had been through, being very poor, divorced, cancer, she could have become bitter and grouchy. But instead, she lets life's struggles roll off her back and lives each day, happy, content and a pleasure to be around. She's a survivor!

Her mild-mannered approach to life carries over to her investment philosophy as well. The IRA account statement she brought for my review showed the half dozen mutual funds selected for her by her prior advisor. One of the funds had done quite well over the years and she was fond of it for that reason. The other funds she had no particular knowledge of, or attachment to. She wasn't interested in spending her days reading over fund prospectuses or worrying over the day-to-day ups and downs of the funds. She had more precious ways to spend her time. This approach is wonderful and the proper mindset I address in Chapter 9, Creating Wealth and Abundance.

I prepared an analysis of her IRA investments and walked her through it, pointing out the strengths and weaknesses. I also gave her a side-by-side comparison of her portfolio versus one of my own managed portfolios and explained to her how my dynamic approach to asset allocation works. You will find information about my approach to investing in Appendix 1.

The other thing I did for Patricia in one of these early meetings was to prepare a retirement cash-flow projection—all the way out to age 100. This projection showed that she would never have to worry about running out of money. I think of it as a blueprint or roadmap. As long as she stays within a defined standard of living, she will be fine. More than fine, really, because it shows that she has considerable flexibility to cover travel, home improvements and such.

Patricia was quite satisfied with my retirement cash-flow projection and my approach to money management. She asked that we move forward with the plan and my management of her IRA. I could tell that she knew what she wanted. She knew she had choices to make and she made them. She wanted someone to manage her IRA investments and she wanted someone she could lean on for financial advice. She didn't want to be doing this on her own, so she needed someone she could trust.

She didn't dwell on investment performance expectations and demand that her portfolio beat the S&P 500 Index. She just wanted to maintain her lifestyle, meet her financial objectives and not worry about money. After all, increasing her wealth wouldn't buy her more happiness.

Making it Happen

Here are some thoughts for your consideration, after having read Patricia's story and my perspective on it. Each step or puzzle piece I share here is related to Patricia and her circumstances one way or another. What's important, of course, is for you to see what you can learn from Patricia to assist you in making your life more happy and secure.

The Happy Retirement Revealed

Michelangelo insisted that he never created his glorious statues—he simply revealed them. His only talent, he said, was in looking at the block of marble and discerning the statue within. All he then needed was the skill to chip away the excess, letting the statue emerge. That is what this chapter will help you do: identify your outlook about retirement, reveal what your retirement might look like, and help you give yourself permission to retire—or not—in your own style and as you see fit.

I'm certain Patricia is enjoying her retirement to the fullest. Knowing her, she's probably photographing a vineyard somewhere in Sonoma County right now. I'm happy for her.

What kind of retirement do you think you'll have? An outstanding one? A depressing one? What if it all starts with your outlook? Qualitatively speaking, what if the success or failure of your retirement begins with your perception of retirement?

A whole field of study has emerged on the psychology of saving, spending and investing: Behavioral Finance. Since retirement saving is a behavior (and since other behaviors influence it), it is worth considering ways to adjust those behaviors and presumptions to encourage a better retirement.

 Delayed gratification or instant gratification? Many people close to retirement age would take the latter over the former. Is that a good choice? Often, it isn't. Financially speaking, retiring early has its drawbacks and may lead you into the next phase of your life with less income and savings. You'll find in Chapter 3 that Betty regretted retiring as early as she did—she's short on cash now.

 If you don't love what you do for a living, you may see only the downside of working longer, rather than the potential boost it could provide to your retirement planning. For example, you may claim Social Security later, tapping retirement account balances later and letting them compound more. If you see work as a daily set of unfulfilling tasks and retirement as an endless Saturday, Saturday will win out and your mindset will lead you to retire earlier with less money. Perhaps instead of thinking about retirement you should be looking for a new job! As I've been saying, you have choices.

On the other hand, if you change your outlook to associate working longer with retiring more comfortably, you may leave work later with a bigger retirement nest egg—and who wouldn't want that?

 Resist the temptation to claim Social Security early. While some retirees claim Social Security at age 62 out of necessity, others do so out of inclination, perhaps not realizing that inflation pressures and long term care costs may render that a poor decision in the long run. There are software programs available which will calculate your optimal Social Security claiming strategy. This calculation can boost your benefit by tens of thousands of dollars. Running it for yourself may make you happy and secure. I'll even run a complementary report for you, as I mention later.

The good news is that Americans are waiting longer to claim Social Security than they once did. Providing your health and employment hold up and you can work longer, patience can lead you to have more Social Security income rather than less. If you claim Social Security prior to reaching what they consider full retirement age, you will be receiving a lesser amount. But if you defer claiming benefits until after your full retirement age, you will receive an 8% increase for each year you defer, up to age 70.

Take a step back from your own experience. For some perspective on what your retirement might be like, consider the lives of others. You undoubtedly know some retirees; think about how their retirements have gone. Who planned well and who didn't? What happened that was unexpected? Financial professionals and other consultants to retirees can also share ideas, as they have seen numerous retirements unfold.

 Reduce your debt. Rather than assume new consumer debts, as advertisers encourage you to do to "keep up" with your salary and career growth, pay down your debts as best you can with the outlook that you are leaving yourself more money for the future (or for unexpected situations).

 Save and invest consistently. See if you can increase your savings rate enroute to retirement. Don't look at it as stripping money out of your present. Look at it as giving yourself a present, the gift of investing for a more comfortable retirement. In essence, this is the storyline of *The Richest Man in Babylon*, a book listed in the Financial Independence Resources section.

Retirement: Define it and Live it!

How do you know if your retirement is living up to its potential? There isn't a standard definition of a successful retirement. (Maybe there should be, but there isn't.) It is interesting to see how different people define it. Patricia, by all of her own standards, is living the dream.

Maybe income is the yardstick. Make that income replacement. A recent article in *Financial Advisor* Magazine put it this way: "Successful retirement is defined as the ability to replace current income in retirement." The Employee Benefit Research Institute (EBRI), which tracks workplace retirement savings trends in America, defines retirement success in similar, if narrower, terms. To EBRI, "success" equals a combination of Social Security income and 401(k) savings that replace 80% of preretirement income after adjusting for inflation.

 Maybe health matters most. Perhaps a successful retirement means successful aging—staving off mental and physical decline. In a poll of 768 non-retired investors conducted for the John Hancock Financial Network, 49% of respondents said being healthy best signifies retirement success. (Just 27% said having enough income represented success.) While we'd all like to feel like we are 30 when we reach 80, MarketWatch's Elizabeth O'Brien notes that physical and mental independence shouldn't be the only definition of successful aging: "We lionize the person living alone at 95, and while that's certainly laudatory, we could also celebrate those who remain connected to their communities despite their infirmities, or those who have saved enough to afford whatever care is needed."

 Maybe our capacity to make a difference or to grow matters most. We can make the most of our "second act" in many ways—through service, through adventure, through learning, or leaving a legacy. Many baby boomers expect nothing less. The vast majority of my clients have some kind of 'give back' gene. They want to get involved with a charitable board, or find ways to be a teacher or tutor. Patricia's favorite charity to volunteer with is the American Cancer Society, specifically their Relay for Life fundraiser. Which one would be yours?

A successful retirement is ultimately one that meets your expectations. Within months or years after you retire, you will probably reflect on how things are proceeding—and if your retirement looks something like the life you had in mind or the life you planned for, then you can call it a success.

Income Tax Planning—IRA Distribution vs. Withdrawal from Brokerage Accounts

 Income tax is an issue for Patricia, because she breathes and there's an IRS—right? Seriously, all of Patricia's sources of income are taxable. She can pull money out of her IRA to supplement her CalSTRS pension. Both are taxable. If she had a brokerage account, that would be another source of cash when needed, but she doesn't have this. If you do, you have options.

Anyone who needs a sum of money, to make a purchase for example, should explore all options before taking the money from an IRA or a brokerage account. The question of where to take the money from is not always as simple as selling the stock with the least gain. Some people may benefit more by taking advantage of the lower capital gains rate. Others may benefit more by taking withdrawals from an IRA. Keep in mind the early withdrawal penalties on IRAs if you're under age 59 ½.

Higher tax brackets. Taxpayers whose income is subject to higher tax brackets may want to avoid taking IRA distributions because these are taxed at ordinary income rates. Instead, taxpayers in this category will benefit from capital gains or even capital losses, which can be achieved from a brokerage account, but not an IRA.

Lower tax brackets. Taxpayers whose income is subject to little or no income tax (due to little or no taxable income and/or personal exemptions and the standard deduction), should consider withdrawals from an IRA to generate additional funds. By carefully calculating the withdrawal amount, taxpayers may be able to remove money from IRAs while paying little or no income tax on the withdrawals. Also, because the capital gains tax rate is favorable, taxpayers may benefit by paying a reduced rate on capital gains realized through the sale of capital assets.

Possible risks:

- When taking distributions from IRAs or doing conversions, careful calculations must be made to ensure taxpayers do not create taxable income. Social Security payments could become taxable if income from other sources is too high.

- Taxpayers making IRA withdrawals early in a tax year based on this strategy may find some unintended consequences if the strategy is changed later in the year. For example, a taxpayer who removes more money from an IRA later in the year may find his or her Social Security being subject to tax. Or, the taxpayer may cause some or all of the capital gain taken earlier in the year to now become taxable.

Key Takeaways

- Identify your outlook about retirement, giving yourself permission to retire—or not—in your own style and as you see fit.

- See if you can increase your savings rate enroute to retirement. Don't look at it as stripping money out of your present. Look at it as giving yourself a present, the gift of investing for a more comfortable retirement.

- Social Security optimization can put tens of thousands of dollars in your pocket. If you would like, I'll run a complementary report for you. See the free resources page at the end of the book.

- You should explore all options and look at the tax consequences before taking money from an IRA or a brokerage account. The question of where to take the money from is not always as simple as selling the stock with the least gain.

- A successful retirement is ultimately one that meets your expectations. Define it and live it!

Chapter 2

Don't Worry — Be Happy

We had a sudden reduction in income. I tried hiding how desperate I was feeling from my wife. Eventually, I realized that we needed the help of a financial advisor.

John and Amanda's Story

I met my wife, Amanda, when I was a flight instructor in Visalia. Her father frequently rented planes from where I worked, so I spent a lot of time with him before he felt that I was worthy of meeting his daughter. I was the only one of my buddies brave enough to give her my number—and the rest is history! She mellows out my excitable tendencies, and she gets me to see different perspectives on everything. When we had a happy accident, our first and only child, a son, we were happier than ever but we did struggle. I was always on the search for the "magic job," and that search took us all over California and even all the way to Chicago. After years of searching I was hired as a pilot for a major airline, and we could finally settle ourselves in one place, Sonoma County, with a steady flow of income.

Amanda's great, and I love her with all my heart, but the one thing she has never been good at is numbers. Neither have I, for that matter, but I was the one who constantly worried about money in our family. Every month I'd give her a little briefing on how much we had for spending money after all the bills were paid. If she overspent, I'd find some way to cover for it, like working more hours, things like that. At one point, the airline I worked for went through bankruptcy and I took a huge pay cut. I had to start working as a realtor and a fishing guide as well as working as a pilot, and with Amanda's two jobs and our son's two jobs we managed to get through the tough times. I was no stranger to hard work; I'd worked hard since age eight, when I swept the parking lot of my parents' store for 50¢ a night. However, our sudden change in lifestyle was really hard on both me and Amanda, although we reacted in very different ways. She couldn't stop spending the way she was used to, and I stopped looking closely at our finances while trying not to let on to Amanda how desperate I felt. Although my employer, a large airline company, started to recover from the bankruptcy, I knew we had to move a chunk of my retirement fund somewhere else. I tried managing our money myself, but it's impossible to do well if you don't have boatloads of time on your hands to watch the market every day. Finally, I suggested to Amanda that we get a financial advisor.

I'd had a guy in mind, but Amanda suggested we shop around for someone both of us could really like and trust with our money. We finally found the perfect financial advisor for us, and at that first meeting where he laid out exactly what documents he needed to see and what he could do for us, we were so glad we came. Getting all our documents together wasn't so much difficult as detailed, but in a good way; it forced us to look at our lives under a microscope and plug up the holes where money was concerned. When we finally had the meeting where he laid out our retirement plan, I felt like a huge weight was lifted off my shoulders. On the car ride home, we just couldn't stop saying, "I'm so happy and relieved at where we are now," and "We're a lot better off than I thought."

Having that plan in place still feels great months later, and I don't worry nearly as much as I used to. Seeing Monty also helped me and Amanda get on the same page about our finances. A lot of people I talk to are reluctant to get an advisor because of the fees, but the fees

14

are worth the peace of mind that comes with having a professional plan in place. If I ever find myself having doubts I just look at how much I'd have to lose versus gain if I tried to go back to doing it myself. I think financial planning is one of the most important things you can do; lots of people lose sleep over their financial worries, but it's just not necessary when there are professionals out there who can take care of everything for you.

The Advisor's Perspective

John and Amanda were referred to me by another CPA in town. Prior to coming in to see me, John had read my book, *Before It's Too Late: Retirement & Estate Solutions*. He seemed to have loved the book and my financial planning strategies and was anxious to get started.

In our client questionnaire, John answered the question: "What expectations do you have of our firm?" He wrote, "To provide honest answers—no B.S." This of course made me laugh. It is a good answer, although I like to think honesty goes without saying. Oh, but I realize there are those wolves out there in sheep's clothing. See Chapter 7 for information on choosing the right advisor.

On the questionnaire, where I ask "What keeps you up at night?" John wrote, "Government policies and job stability in the airline industry!" I do see government policy as a growing concern. Many clients express their concern over government policy and what it will do to their future and that of their children. While it is difficult to protect yourself from every unpleasant potential contingency, there are many steps we can take to minimize the impact of the uncertainty which lies ahead. Of course, the first step is to create a comprehensive financial plan. More on this later.

With regard to John's worry about job stability, I see this as a real and present danger as well. I have baby boomer clients who have great jobs with great companies and they're relying on their ability to stay with that company for X number of years as they scramble to boost their retirement preparedness. This, however, is not something they can be assured of. The economy is fragile and companies seldom care that their corporate restructuring decisions don't coincide with your retirement plans. Here again, you need a financial plan in place.

It is not typical that the husband is the one who expresses worry about money—usually it is the wife. In my experience, men are generally the risk takers, and women seem more security minded. Well, not in this case. John was worried, so they sought help and came in for planning. It really helped relieve his anxiety. It also improved his and Amanda's communication about their financial picture and united them and their goals. A great outcome! Worrying is not productive. Taking action and making a financial plan is the easy and smart choice.

Worry was the first indicator that they had NO plan. In my initial review of their situation, I noticed John certainly had plenty of cause for worry. They had no cash reserve to speak of, no long term care insurance and inadequate life insurance. They had consumer debt of about $42,000. They had no estate documents. John's employer was going through bankruptcy. There were decisions to be made about his company pension plan. And Amanda didn't even really know about all this.

John and Amanda's situation, both financially and in terms of being worried or discouraged, is actually common these days. According to the results of a recent Washington Post-Miller Center poll exploring Americans' changing definition of success and their confidence in the country's future, five years into an economic recovery the majority still believe that the American Dream is becoming markedly more elusive.

While most Americans still think hard work and education breeds opportunity, their faith in a brighter tomorrow has been eroded by intensifying struggles on the job and at home. This has led some to conclude that the U.S. has emerged from the Great Recession a fundamentally changed nation.

Three of the poll's findings stick out: 1) one in three say their money worries are with them all or most of the time, 2) more than six in ten workers worry they will lose their jobs because of the economy, and 3) almost eight in ten Americans say they worry they won't have enough saved for retirement.

I'd like to suggest that all those survey respondents read the introduction to this book. America is the land of opportunity! If you haven't found yours yet, that is okay. Don't give up. It may be just around the next corner.

Wiping Out the Worry

Let's delve into John and Amanda's situation so you can see what they were dealing with. John is 52 and plans to work another 13 years. Amanda is 50 and currently not employed outside of the home. John has been employed many years with an airline company, earning $115,000 annually, and the company's pension plan offers a lifetime payout of $48,000 per year starting at age 65. His Social Security benefit at age 67 would be $30,000 per year, and Amanda's benefit at age 67 would be $14,000 per year. They have one child, age 25, who is self-supporting.

What They Own and What They Owe	
John's Company Retirement Fund	$402,000
John's Company 401(k)	$245,000
Amanda's IRA	$16,000
Home	$520,000
Home Mortgage	($305,000)
Consumer Debt	($20,000)
John's 401(k) Loan	($22,000)
Net-Worth	$836,000

John and Amanda's Financial Objectives
1. Retire in 2025 with at least $72,000 of guaranteed annual retirement income (this will be $100,000 in 2025 dollars).
2. Take an in-service distribution and rollover John's retirement funds to gain control and have more investment choice (even though he is under age 59 ½, this is an option he has due to a company merger in process).
3. Get their estate documents in order.
4. Increase their cash reserve fund.
5. Reduce their stock market anxiety.
6. Fill as many gaps in their financial pyramid as possible.

The first step of my financial planning process, which I call the Wealth Integration Review, is to map John and Amanda's financial resources into the various blocks of my Peace of Mind Retirement planning pyramid.

(For a basic explanation of this pyramid concept, see Appendix 2.)

Here is What I Discovered in Examining Their Pyramid
1. Too much of their wealth was concentrated in the "Growth Investments" peak of the pyramid.
2. They had an insufficient "Uninterrupted Pension System" (UPS) to provide guaranteed lifetime income, especially since they were anxious about the stock market and wanted more certainty.
3. John was vigorously saving for retirement, but it was creating a "Tax Bomb" in their future.
4. Their house was not titled to a living trust—an error which could have cost their estate $15,000 in probate fees.
5. They had no living trust, wills, power of attorney or healthcare directives.
6. They had no long term care insurance.
7. John was over-paying for an inadequate life insurance policy.
8. They have $215,000 in home equity earning zero percent rate of return.

With some repositioning of assets and "fixing" their pyramid, I could see how their financial objectives could be realized. I suggested a shift of some of their assets from stock market investments into a pension system for guaranteed income, what I call UPS, in order to reduce their stock market anxiety and increase their retirement certainty. I recommended that they increase their cash reserve fund and also pay off all consumer debts. I suggested that John make future retirement savings contributions to a structured life insurance contract with a long term care rider. This would help reduce the "Tax Bomb" in their future and provide a different type of bucket of cash to be accessed in different ways—non-taxable ways. Please note: there is nothing "cookie-cutter" about this plan! It is completely driven by their goals, not product-driven in any sense.

"Tax Bomb" is how I refer to the huge taxation that happens upon the eventual withdrawal of your tax-deferred retirement accounts and the resultant sharing of your hard-earned retirement fund with Uncle Sam. You can read more about the "Tax Bomb" in a White Paper I've written. See the free resources page at the end of the book.

To illustrate how the elements of their plan work together, I ran a Retirement Cash Flow projection for John and Amanda. The projection showed year by year income from each source and compared it with annual living expenses, building in an inflation factor to maintain their standard of living. It also showed their growth and/or depletion of assets, year by year. Since it was run all the way out to their life expectancy, they could see if their worry about running out of money was warranted or not. With this projection, John and Amanda knew what their financial future would look like and that helped them make better decisions. In John and Amanda's case, it showed that they were well on their way to a happy and secure retirement. They had flexibility and were in control. I continued to help by updating their projection periodically.

You can get a printed copy of John and Amanda's Retirement Cash Flow projection by following the instructions on the free resources page at the end of the book. I also offer my Net Worth Planning Worksheet, available as an Excel spreadsheet.

When John and Amanda first came in they were nervous and uncertain about their financial future. Going through this planning process reassured them and gave them the ability to make sound financial and retirement decisions today.

Making it Happen

Financial Planning

 When you do financial planning you're looking toward your future, specifically at building the financial security you'd like to have and assuring you'll be able to afford the life you want to live. But to plan successfully, you also have to evaluate your present, including the financial choices you're making now. Otherwise it's too easy to find yourself making random decisions that won't move you toward your goals effectively, or that may even interfere with achieving your goals. That is where John found himself. He was making random financial moves in the present, but they weren't helping his anxiety or securing his and Amanda's future.

It's never too soon, or too late, to begin. Financial planning is important, whether you've just started working or are thinking seriously about retirement. And it should be an on-going process, revising your goals and updating your strategies.

Without planning, you run greater financial risks. You may not have enough money in reserve to meet expenses you're expecting, like the down payment on a home or the price of a college education. You may have to revise your retirement plans. Or you might leave your family without enough to live comfortably if something happens to you.

Planning Strategies

 In financial planning terms, creating a financial strategy means defining the steps you'll take to have the money you need to pay for the things you want.

To begin, you need a clear sense of your goals, and what they will cost. You have to evaluate the assets you already have and find ways to increase the amount you're saving and investing. While planning doesn't guarantee success, failure to plan is likely to bring disappointment. Notice how I helped John and Amanda determine and write down their financial objectives. This is the first step.

Wealth Integration Review

The very wealthy likely have an entire team of professionals helping them with their money, right? If you were Bill Gates, you would have a group of highly paid consultants, including an investment specialist, a banker, a mortgage broker, an estate planning attorney, a CPA, and an insurance guru all sitting around the table to help you manage your money. I am sure it costs Bill thousands of dollars every time they all get together to coordinate his affairs.

I feel that everyone facing retirement needs this same type of coordinated financial advice, because the world has gotten just too darn complicated. That's why I created our Wealth Integration Review process, to help individuals just like John and Amanda get the kind of coordinated advice that was previously only available to the very wealthy. That's what we do in a Wealth Integration Review—we provide a coordinated team of experts to help people like you, who are in or nearing retirement, manage all aspects of their financial life. And you won't pay what Bill Gates pays!

I recently delivered one of these coordinated plans to a single woman who is hoping to retire in nine years. I went through the plan document page by page, discussing each implementation action step, ensuring she understood and agreed with each step. At the end, she was very happy. She said, *"I feel like a huge weight has just been lifted off my shoulders!"* This is pretty much the same thing John and Amanda said to me when their plan was implemented.

This is where I find joy in doing what I do, knowing that we have a team assembled who can deliver peace of mind to people facing financial uncertainty—people who just want to enjoy life, free from worry about money.

So, I have a question for you: **If you're only going to work for 40 years and then retire once in your lifetime, why settle for ordinary retirement planning?**

Patti Gribow described my holistic team approach to reviewing and integrating my clients' financial affairs as "beautiful" and the kind of service she wants for herself. Patti and I had many such discussions leading up to the filming of her interview with me on the Patti Gribow

Show, aired on the Comcast Hometown Channel. (Who is Patti Gribow? Years ago, Patti Pivarnik Gribow was the Captain of the Golddiggers dance team on the Dean Martin Show! Now, she is the host of her own show, The Patti Gribow Show, where she interviews people who are making an impact on the global community.) I mention this because I respect her opinion, as a well-connected person who interviews a lot of people.

Our Wealth Integration Review service is extraordinary. It's the Cadillac.

Income Tax Planning — 401(k) Loans

 John had borrowed money from his 401(k) plan and I warned him of the risk he was taking. John's employer, the airline company, was in bankruptcy and John was talking about finding a new job. Here are some of the risks involved:

- The biggest risk of a 401(k) loan is loss of employment. If John leaves his job, outstanding loan balances must be paid back, generally within 60 days. If the loan is not paid back, it is considered a distribution and is taxable. Since John is under age 59 ½ and does not qualify for an exception, a 10% early distribution penalty also applies.

- Another risk is that of lost opportunity. While the money from a 401(k) is out on loan, it is not invested in the stock or bond funds of the 401(k). This can generate smaller returns for the investor, especially if the returns of those funds are substantial.

- You may be eligible for a loan that has tax deductible interest, such as a home equity loan or a business loan. You should seek other loan options based on the purpose of the loan.

While many pitfalls do exist, a 401(k) loan can still be a viable option depending on your situation. For some, it may be the only source of funds, especially in times of emergencies. The issue of taking a loan from a 401(k) is controversial among advisors, probably because we see people taking these loans when there are better alternatives or when they do not understand the risks.

Key Takeaways

- John and Amanda worried needlessly. Their worry went away once they sat down with a wealth advisor. Don't hesitate to get the help you need.

- Financial planning is important and it's never too soon, or too late, to begin.

- If you would like help in projecting and growing your net worth, you may request a copy of my Net Worth Planning Worksheet in Excel. See the Free Resources page at the end of the book.

- If you would like a simple but helpful one-page financial planning worksheet, you may request a copy of *Where Are You Today?* See the Free Resources page at the end of the book.

- If you would like to see a sample of my Retirement Cash Flow Calculation projection, you may request one. See the Free Resources page at the end of the book.

- Read more about the "Tax Bomb" you may be creating in your 401(k). See the Free Resources page at the end of the book.

- Bill Gates probably has a team of professionals helping him integrate his financial planning. You need one too. In fact, it could be argued that you need one even more than he does.

- You should think of a 401(k) loan as the last resort. Look carefully, as there are probably better alternatives.

Chapter 3

Retirement as a Single Woman

As a divorced woman, I raised my two children on my own. That was challenging enough and, of course, I had no retirement plan. Now that I am retired, I can think of things that I wish I did differently.

Betty's Story

I got married right out of high school—never a great idea. I was a baby still, and trying to take care of my own baby was very difficult; I had no idea what I was doing. That marriage ended in divorce before too long, before my first child was even born, but I remarried fairly quickly. I was prepared to take care of all the bill paying, but my husband didn't like that and he decided to take it over. However, he only paid about $10 of each bill so he'd have more money for himself! I wasn't working at the time, so I didn't have any money of my own to speak of until my mother suggested I take the change from the grocery money he gave me and stash it in a savings account. It came to a point where we just couldn't resolve our issues, and we knew we had to get a divorce. We sat down and split up the home equity and most other things, but he took both of our cars and refused to pay child support. He also left me with a terrible credit rating and massive amounts of debt to pay off. That was when I knew I had to get out and never look back.

With the little bit of savings I had managed to accumulate, I took my kids (by this time I had two) to Southern California and moved in with my cousin. I knew I had to get a job, and after brushing up my typing, shorthand, and dictation, I was able to land a position as a secretary. My cousin and I had different parenting strategies, so eventually we had to part ways. I got my own apartment with my kids in a really poor neighborhood. Even though we didn't have much, those days were some of the best of my life. We didn't have enough money to buy Christmas presents, so my kids and I made each other our gifts, and we became really close as we found new—and free!— ways to have fun together. Sadly, I lost sight of that once I started to move upward at my job. At that point we finally had some money but I was extremely focused on the now rather than saving up or planning ahead. One of my biggest regrets was that I racked up a bit of credit card debt because it was just so easy to charge everything. It was the juggling act of having kids—I'd go from Christmas costs to dentist appointments to new school clothes hoping that I'd be able to pay everything off before the next big thing came up, and I didn't plan ahead very well. I also didn't go into my job having any sort of plan to save for retirement; I was just living day to day trying to put dinner on the table for my kids. I regret not doing more with my kids back then; I'd just get so exhausted after work. But I'd always try to remember what my parents taught me about work: give 120% to the company at work, but leave work in the office, physically and mentally, at the end of the day.

When my kids were grown, I got an offer for a big promotion in Sonoma County, so I decided to move up north and take it. My biggest challenge at that point was figuring out who I was outside of being a mom. I had to make my own decisions and make it on my own, and shift my focus from my kids to my career. Now that my kids were starting to have their own lives, my thoughts turned to the future and I realized I had no plan. A man I worked with sort of took me under his wing and helped me figure out how to save as much as I could from each paycheck, and following his advice was probably the smartest move I made financially. As a single mom, you tend to focus on getting through the day and taking care of your kids, but now I had to start thinking of the future and retirement. I took some classes and met with a few financial advisors and investment firms, and eventually I had a portfolio that assured me I could retire at 61.

In retirement I've made sure to take out some long term care insurance, but I've also been careful to not make myself insurance poor. I've spent my time in retirement getting to know my grandkids as people and expanding on my talent as a painter; I never wanted to travel, which is partly why I could retire early. Even though I've loved retirement, the one regret I have is that I didn't save much of a safety net. If I could do it again, I'd probably work another couple years for just a bit of extra security to account for the changing economy and unexpected expenses. But truly, retirement and success in general aren't just about finances, they're about the people in your life-and I've used my retirement to the fullest to appreciate the ones I love.

The Advisor's Perspective

Betty was referred to me in 2005 by one of my existing clients. She told me that she was becoming more and more uncomfortable with her current financial advisor. He had the practice of asking her to periodically swap one annuity for another annuity. Betty was not sure if this was a wise idea. She told me that she would raise her concerns to him, but he was such a smooth talker that he would convince her that everything was fine and then give her a big hug on the way out the door. She felt fine, until she got home and she felt horrible.

Her financial advisor was putting on dinner seminars every month here in Santa Rosa at the Hungry Hunter Steakhouse. He also had a house up in Tahoe he would loan out to his clients on occasion. He had quite the name in town for a while—while it lasted. Betty wasn't the only client of his who came running to me for help. One interesting thing was that his ex-wife even transferred some accounts of hers over to me! When you do a google search on him now, you can't find him working anywhere as an advisor.

One of the things that popped out to me when I reviewed Betty's accounts was that some listed her two children as equal beneficiaries and other accounts were filled in with "As Per Trust." Betty told me that this is the way the advisor filled it in and she was relying on his expertise. Obviously, he didn't understand or care what kind of a mess he was creating.

Here's the problem: one of Betty's children is disabled and receiving government benefits. If he were to directly inherit any of these accounts, this would interfere with the government benefits and put more money in his hands than he is capable of managing. I reviewed Betty's living trust and found that it was not a proper IRA conduit trust. I explained all of this to Betty and followed it up with a four page letter for her to take to her attorney.

Betty's attorney, at a long-standing law firm in Santa Rosa, informed her that the charge to make these changes would be a couple thousand dollars. Betty didn't feel she should have to pay the attorney to fix an error they had made in drafting the trust, and therefore, she was looking for a new attorney. I spoke with an estate planning attorney friend of mine, Teresa Norton, and received a very reasonable quote to draft a trust amendment fixing all the issues I had raised. Betty and I met with Teresa Norton and got it all resolved. Betty was amazed by how thorough I was and that I took the time to attend attorney meetings to ensure that she was being taken care of properly. I told her this was just normal business for me.

I'm happy to report that Betty is enjoying her retirement here in Sonoma County and loves all the time she can get with her grandkids. She finds joy in her sense of humor, painting, quilting and her relationship with Christ.

Making it Happen

A Woman's Financial Plan — After Divorce

 You have just gone through one of the most challenging and difficult periods that a woman can experience in her life—a divorce. While many things may still be up in the air, one aspect of your life that you should make sure you're in control of is your finances. I am, of course, not advocating for divorce—just speaking to the reality of it and hoping this may be helpful. I know that getting control of her finances was one of Betty's highest priorities, because her ex-husband was so controlling over their bank accounts.

Financial planning for divorced women is not much different from financial planning for married couples. Several basic elements are the same. However, the differences offer both good news and bad news. The good news: it's all in your hands. You can make plans and decisions based solely on your needs and goals. There won't be miscommunication or conflicting ideas. The bad news: it's all in your hands. Any mistakes will be your own and a poor decision can't be salvaged by the income or assets of a partner.

One way to counter the bad news is to find and seek advice from a trusted professional.

After a divorce, friends are often split between spouses. Financial advisors can be the same way. If you lost yours in the divorce or never had one to begin with, it's a good time to consider finding a professional who can help you make sound financial decisions for your new life. To find one, start simply. Ask friends or acquaintances who helped them when they went through a divorce. The attorney who handled your divorce may also be a good source for a referral. Selecting the right professional for you is a critical step. After all, this person will be helping you with the important financial decisions you now have to face. See Chapter 7 for a list of questions you should ask a prospective advisor.

Long term care insurance may become even more important post-divorce.

Long term care policies are designed to cover the costs of care if you are unable to care for yourself because of age or if you become ill or disabled. Long term care insurance is especially important for women because they typically pay more for care than men do. The reason is simple: women typically live longer than men and usually require more care during those additional years.

A woman's retirement is usually more expensive than a man's.

The reason that women usually need long term care insurance more than men is the same reason that retirement income planning for women may be more important. Women live on average 5 to 10 years longer than men. Eighty-five percent of people over 100 are women. This means a woman's retirement savings must, on average, be stretched out over a larger number of years. It's important to review your Social Security estimates, any pensions you have and your retirement assets. You can then compare that to the kind of lifestyle you would like to have during retirement. Because a woman's retirement may be more expensive, you may want to make an employer-sponsored retirement plan a larger deciding factor in any job search. Also, you may decide that you must retire at a later date than you had originally planned.

Update your beneficiaries and consider using a trust to help manage your assets.

People often forget to update the beneficiaries of their life insurance and retirement accounts after a divorce. If these are not changed, your ex-husband may stand to inherit a large portion of your assets. Also, estate laws give certain breaks to married couples that are not available to single people. Establishing the proper type of legal trust may be a way to pass along more of your assets to your heirs, rather than to the IRS. This was especially important to Betty, whose disabled son receives government benefits.

Finally, after you have moved on from your divorce, there may come a time when you consider remarriage.

It's important that you understand the financial consequences this may have. If you were married longer than 10 years you may be collecting or entitled to collect 50% of your ex-husband's Social Security benefit. If you remarry you will no longer have that right. While you will become entitled to your new husband's benefit, you must know whether that benefit will be lower or higher, and how that will affect your retirement income.

Remarriage can also lead to blended families, blended assets and blended income. Your new husband may have his own family from a previous relationship. A financial professional can help the two of you prepare for this blending in a way that satisfies the financial needs of each of you, as well as that of your new family.

While it's all in <u>your</u> hands, partnering with a financial professional can help you move on to the next phase of your life with a more solid plan for your financial future.

Beneficiary Designations

 The following represent points from the letter I wrote to Betty—that she shared with her estate attorney. Please keep in mind that I am not an attorney. My comments come from experience in the tax business.

Trusts as IRA Beneficiaries

Trusts as IRA beneficiaries create unique problems and tax complications even when executed perfectly, and that is rare. Any time a trust is named as a beneficiary, you have to follow the distribution rules that apply when you name a non-spouse beneficiary.

A Beneficiary Must Be A Human Being—To Continue the Tax-Deferral Over a Lifetime

The IRA laws say that only a human being can be a 'designated beneficiary' and take out the IRA distributions over a lifetime. A trust is not a person and does not qualify as a 'designated beneficiary' except in one situation. The IRS calls this a "look-through" trust and they will let the IRA pass through the trust and treat the trust beneficiary as if he or she was named directly without a trust. What's at stake? The ability to stretch out the tax-deferral over the life of a beneficiary.

The Five-Year Rule

The trust has to qualify as a designated beneficiary. If the trust fails for some reason to have a designated beneficiary and if you die <u>prior</u> to turning age 70½, then the five-year rule applies. The five-year rule requires the entire inherited IRA to be fully distributed to the beneficiary by the conclusion of the fifth year following your death. It does not matter how much the beneficiary withdraws yearly during the five-year rule period as long as the account is emptied by the end of that period. Any balance remaining in the inherited IRA after that time is subject to the 50 percent penalty.

If you die on or <u>after</u> turning age 70½ and there is no properly designated beneficiary for your IRA, then the IRA will be paid out to your trust over your remaining single life expectancy (per the IRS mortality table) based on your age in the year of death. This means that your intended beneficiaries will not be able to stretch the post-death required distributions over the life expectancy of the oldest beneficiary.

Qualifying the Trust for "Look-Through" Treatment

The trust must meet the following requirements to qualify as a designated beneficiary and allow the life expectancy of the oldest trust beneficiary to be used in calculating postdeath required minimum distributions (RMDs):

- The trust must be a valid trust under state law.

- The trust must be irrevocable at death.

- The beneficiaries of the trust must be identifiable.

- A copy of the trust instrument must be provided to the financial institution with the account by October 31 of the year following the year of your death.

(*Note: The only money that moves from the IRA to the trust are the required distributions, not the whole amount. Moving money out of the IRA triggers immediate taxation.*)

Paying RMDs: From the IRA to the Trust to the Beneficiary

Non-spouse designated beneficiaries get to use their own life expectancies to calculate postdeath RMDs on inherited IRAs, the first of which must be taken by the end of the year after the year of the IRA owner's death. This is the first distribution year, meaning the first year for which the designated beneficiary has a required distribution. Each year thereafter, an RMD must be taken by the end of the year. If an RMD is missed, the 50 percent penalty applies.

Special Needs Trust—Special Problem

Where the trustee has the discretion to accumulate money in the trust, rather than pay it out to the trust beneficiary, those IRA distributions held in the trust will be taxed at trust tax rates rather than at the trust beneficiary's personal income tax rate. Trust rates are higher. ***Planning Point:*** In situations such as this where it is necessary to allow for accumulation in the trust, it is best to convert the IRA to a Roth IRA (if possible). Doing this will completely remove the trust tax problem.

Trust Tax Returns

Another problem with a trust is that after you die, trust tax returns have to be filed each year for the life of the IRA trust. This can lead to possible IRS problems if the IRS decides to audit the trust tax returns. If the returns are selected for audit, the IRA trust will be scrutinized. It better have been correctly drafted, particularly with respect to the IRA tax rules.

Potential Solution #1

You could complete new beneficiary designation forms for all of your IRA accounts, naming your daughter as a 50% Primary Beneficiary and the "Special Needs Trust For The Benefit Of Your Son" as the other 50% Primary Beneficiary—on a "per stirpes" basis. Your daughter's two children could be (by name) Contingent Beneficiaries. (Per stirpes is a Latin term which means that an estate of a decedent is distributed equally to each branch of the family.)

This means that one-half of each of your IRAs would go directly to your daughter as "Inherited IRAs." Your daughter could continue the tax-deferral benefit over her lifetime. If your daughter were to predecease you, then her 50% interests would go to her two children (your grandchildren) as the Contingent Beneficiaries, on a "per stirpes" basis, and they could take it out over their lifetimes.

The other one-half of each of your IRAs would go directly to the special needs trust for your son. With the assistance of your legal counsel, you should consider re-wording the special needs trust to take into account the potential problems outlined above. You may also want to consider converting to a Roth IRA for the purposes of this trust.

Potential Solution #2

Depending on the amount you wish to direct to the special needs trust, you may consider selecting one or more of your current IRAs as specifically designated to fund the trust. In this case you would only name the special needs trust as beneficiary of those particular IRA(s). The other IRA(s) would name your daughter as 100% Primary Beneficiary.

If your current IRA balances don't provide the desired dollar amount, you could split IRAs for the purpose of creating the desired amounts. This would need to be done before your death.

Next Steps

Your current IRA beneficiary designations may be the result of actions taken on your behalf by your prior financial advisor (and believed to be correct) and may not have been reviewed by your legal counsel. It also may not have been the intention of your legal counsel to have the trust named as an IRA beneficiary. You should consult your estate attorney for clarification and correction if needed.

Key Takeaways

- After a divorce, one aspect of your life that you should make sure you're in control of is your finances. This is a good time to get some help.

- While it's all in your hands, partnering with a financial professional can help you move on to the next phase of your life with a more solid plan for your financial future.

- If you would like a simple but helpful one-page financial planning worksheet, you may request a copy of *Where Are You Today?* See the Free Resources page at the end of the book.

- Trusts as IRA beneficiaries create unique problems and tax complications. Rarely is it a good idea to name a family trust as the beneficiary of your retirement account.

- If you have a child who is disabled and receiving government benefits, be very careful that your estate plan does not adversely affect his or her benefits.

Chapter 4

What To Do When A Spouse Dies

It is true, there is nothing certain in life but death and taxes. Even still, I was overwhelmed with uncertainty when my husband died. I should have been better prepared.

Nancy's Story

I already had my own established advertising business when I met my second husband, George. I broke my own rule of not dating clients and fell in love with him! He was a lot older than me, and by the time we were married I was in my 50s and he was in his 60s. He was the one who convinced me to move from Marin County to Sonoma County, a move that I never regretted. George was a "good ole boy" with old-fashioned values, and even though I had my own business and was perfectly capable of handling finances, he stood by the idea that the man should take care of the woman in a marriage and handle the finances. He didn't tell me anything about what was happening with our money, including all of our investments, bills, and even the sale of his own business. I went along with it, even though it went against my desire for independence, because I loved him and I knew he had our best interests at heart.

George did, however, concede to two of my financial requests: hiring a specialist to handle investments and getting long term care insurance. I am extremely grateful for those two things, especially for the long term care insurance. Having that plan in place gave me the reassurance that I wouldn't have to depend on my kids in my old age, but it became even more essential than I could have imagined when George had his stroke. He lost his verbal abilities and life became a lot harder physically, emotionally, and financially. I don't know how I did it, but I managed to work while George was sick, so at least we had a bit of income from that. But the hardest financial challenge I faced during that time was trying to figure out what was going on with our finances. George could only nod or make small gestures when I asked him questions, so I had to do a lot of detective work to figure out what was going on with the sale of his business and all our investments and bills. When he passed away, my whole world was rocked. We'd been married for 9 years and 10 months, and going back to life on my own after all that time was one of the biggest challenges I ever faced. I was just grateful for the long term care insurance—it saved my financial life during my time of need. I needed the reassurance now more than ever that my death wouldn't leave my kids financially crippled. I've seen that sort of thing tear families apart, and I will not let my kids fight over me; I've always taken pride in my independence from others, financially and otherwise. I also know I will never have to eat dog food like some of the elders I knew growing up because I've lived my life independently and I know I'll be able to provide for myself when I get old. I was grateful that it turned out that our estate planning documents were in order—a big relief. It took me three years to finally fully face dealing with our investments. During those three years I really didn't do much with our money; I couldn't bring myself to make any big decisions or changes, and I just focused on living day to day.

If I have one piece of advice for married couples, it's to always be partners. Both people in the marriage need to know what's going on with the finances, because the day will come when one person in the marriage will have to take on all of that on their own. I would've felt a lot more prepared for George's death. Also, long term care insurance and estate planning are essential. It's just foolish to be an ostrich with your head in the sand about these things!

The Advisor's Perspective

I had known Nancy for a few years, as a vendor to my business, prior to the passing of her husband. She had been telling me that she'd like me to handle the preparation of their income tax returns. That didn't happen until her husband died and her tax needs became more challenging.

This, of course, was a traumatic time in her life. It is a common event for women since they generally outlive their husbands, but knowing this doesn't help the grieving process. It's traumatic—I've counseled grieving widows countless times over the years so I know.

I met with Nancy shortly after her husband died. We took care of the tax filing issues. Nancy also asked me to manage $200,000 which she had just received from a life insurance death benefit claim. I also sat in on a meeting with Nancy, her estate attorney and her investment advisor. That was all of the help she wanted at that time. She kept herself busy with her job.

I only saw Nancy during tax time for the next three years. Even though she received an investment report from me every quarter with an invitation to come in for a review meeting, she never once came in. Close to the end of those three years, she attended a seminar I taught on Retirement and Estate Solutions. After that seminar she finally came in to discuss something beyond taxes.

She shared that it took that much time to be able to deal with the loss of her husband and prepare herself to move on with her life. During those three years she didn't really make financial decisions, make changes, or do anything big . . . just lived day to day. In the seminar, I suggested to the attendees that they come into my office for a comprehensive financial evaluation—a Wealth Integration Review.

Nancy said she was now ready for our Wealth Integration Review. This review is conducted by our team, consisting of an estate attorney, an insurance expert, a CPA and an Investment Advisor, all in the room at one time with the client. We discussed all of Nancy's financial issues: her real estate holdings, her insurance policies, Social Security, retirement preparedness, estate documentation, income tax reduction strategy, investment performance and guaranteed lifetime income. Nancy brought her daughter and son-in-law to the meeting with her for extra support, which I encouraged.

> I won't go into more detail of our Wealth Integration Review (WIR) process here or the cost for this service. You can refer back to Chapter 2 regarding the WIR. You can also receive a report on it for further reading. See the Free Resources page at the end of the book.

By this time, Nancy's investment with me had grown to $264,000. She realized that it would be more beneficial for her to consolidate all of her investments under my management. This was not an easy decision, as she had her other investment advisor in place for many years and liked him very much. Again, choices to be made. But when she compared what I was capable of doing for her—and in fact was doing for her—she made the decision to place all of her investments with me. She understood how thorough my management process was and could now see where her other investment accounts were coming up short.

Making it Happen

Step by Step, First Things First

 When a spouse passes away, the emotion and magnitude of the loss can send our lives reeling, as it did with Nancy. This profound change can also affect our finances. All at once, we have a to-do list before us, and the responsibility of it can make us feel pressured. With that in mind, these guidelines are intended as a kind of checklist—a list of some of the key financial matters to address following the death of a spouse.

The first steps. These actions should come as soon as you are able. Some of these steps require locating some documentation. Hopefully, your spouse kept these documents where you can easily find them—either at home, in a safe deposit box or in an online vault.

1. Contact family members, friends and your spouse's employer to tell them of your spouse's passing. (As a courtesy, your spouse's employer should put you in touch with the person overseeing its employee benefits plan or Human Resources Department.)

2. If your spouse owned a business, check to see what plans are in place for its short term continuation. Will a partner or key employee take the reins for the time being (or for the long term) as a result of a defined succession plan?

3. Arrange payment for funeral expenses, and don't forget to look for veteran's benefits or pre-paid burial plan documents.

4. Gather/request as many records as you can find to document your spouse's life and passing—birth and death certificates, a marriage certificate or divorce decree (if applicable), military service records, investment, insurance and tax records, and employee benefit information (if applicable).

The next steps. Subsequently, it is time to talk with the legal, tax, insurance and financial professionals you trust.

1. Consult your attorney. Assuming your spouse left a will and did not die intestate (i.e., without one), that will should be looked at before the distribution of any assets and the settlement of the estate. Your spouse's written wishes should be reviewed.

2. Locate your spouse's life insurance policy and talk to your insurance agent. Notify that agent of your spouse's passing; he or she will work with you to a) get the claims process going, b) help you evaluate your own insurance needs, and c) review and perhaps alter future beneficiary designations.

3. Notify your spouse's financial advisor and by extension, the financial custodians (i.e., the banks or investment firms) through which your spouse opened his or her IRAs, money market funds, mutual funds, brokerage accounts, or qualified retirement plan. Account custodians must be notified so that these funds may be properly distributed according to the beneficiary designations for these accounts. Please note that

beneficiary designations commonly take precedence over bequests made in a will. (This is why it is important to periodically review beneficiary designations for all accounts.) If there is no beneficiary form on file with the account custodian, the assets will be distributed according to the custodian's default policy, which often directs assets either to a surviving spouse or to the deceased spouse's estate.

Survivor/spousal benefits. These important benefits may help you to maintain your standard of living after a loss.

1. Contact your local Social Security office regarding Social Security spousal and survivor benefits. Also, visit www.ssa.gov/pgm/survivors.htm online.

2. If your spouse worked in a civil service job or was in the armed forces, contact the state or Federal government branch or armed services branch about filing for survivor benefits.

Your spouse's estate. To settle an estate, several orderly steps should be taken.

1. You and/or your attorney need to contact the executor, trustee(s), guardians and heirs relevant to the estate and review the appropriate estate planning documents.

2. Your attorney can also let you know about the possibility of probate. A revocable living trust (or other estate planning mechanisms) may allow you to avoid this process. Joint tenancy and community property laws in many states also help avoid probate.

3. The executor for the estate needs to determine if any tax returns will be required. If so, an Employer Identification Number (EIN) will need to be obtained from the IRS. Visit: www.irs.gov/businesses/small/article/0,,id=102767,00.html Or, see your tax advisor.

4. Any banks, credit unions and financial firms your spouse had a financial relationship with, which you have not already contacted, should be notified of his or her death.

5. Your spouse's creditors will also need to be informed. Any debts will need to be addressed, and separate credit may need to be established for you.

Your own taxes & investments. How does all of this affect your own financial life?

1. Review the beneficiary designations on the IRAs, workplace retirement plans and insurance policies that are in your name. With the death of a spouse, beneficiary designations will likely have to be revised.
2. Consider your state and federal tax filing status. A change in status may significantly alter your tax picture. You are allowed to file a joint income tax return for the year your spouse died. You may be able to file as a "Qualifying Widow(er)" for the first two years following the year a spouse died, provided you meet the requirements.
3. Speaking of taxes, there may be tax implications surrounding any charitable gifts you and your spouse have recently arranged or planned to make. If a deceased spouse leaves money or property to a surviving spouse or a tax-exempt charity, it is exempt from federal estate tax. Anything gifted by your late spouse during his or her life is not subject to probate.
4. Presuming you jointly owned some assets, it is time to retitle them. In addition to real estate, you may have jointly owned bank accounts, investments and vehicles.
5. For real estate you own jointly, or will otherwise be inheriting, you need to have an appraisal done or at least have a realtor prepare a letter stating the likely fair market value of the property as of the date of death. This is very important so that you can substantiate the step up in basis which is allowed and will minimize your tax in the future.

Things to think about when you are ready to move forward. With the passage of time, you may need to give some thought to the short term *and* long term financial and lifestyle consequences of your spouse's passing.

1. Some widowed spouses ponder selling a home or moving to be closer to adult children in such circumstances, but this is not always the clearest moment to make such decisions.

2. Think about your own retirement planning needs. Certainly, you had an idea of what your retirement would be like together; to what degree does this life event change that idea? Will potential sources of retirement income need to be replaced?

3. If you have minor children to take care of, will you be able to sustain the family lifestyle on a single income? How do your income sources compare to your fixed and variable expenses?

4. Do you need to address college funding in a new way?

5. If your spouse owned a business or professional practice, to what extent do you want (or need) to be involved in it in the future? Is now a good time to consider selling it or making ownership changes?

The above is intended as a checklist—a list of the important financial considerations to address in the event of a tragedy. **Keep in mind that there are very few things which must be done immediately.** Take your time and don't make irreversible rash decisions.

Income Tax on Inherited Property

 I get many questions from people on this topic and find many are confused about whether or not there is a tax due on an inheritance they receive. Hopefully, the table below will shed some light on this important issue for you.

Taxable	Not Taxable
• Investment income paid after death. • Employer payments—wages, salaries, bonuses, commissions, vacation pay, sick pay. • IRAs (except nondeductible contributions) and SEPs. • Qualified pension plans, profit-sharing plans, deferred compensation. • Annuities (except decedent's investment in the contract). • Accrued interest on Series EE and I bonds unless the decedent paid tax annually. • The gross profit percentage of a contract for deed or other installment sale. • Accounts receivable, partnership interests, S corporation earnings.	• Life insurance proceeds. • Cash, bank accounts, certificates of deposit. • Stocks, bonds, mutual funds (basis changes to fair market value at death). • House, cabin, other real estate (basis changes to fair market value at death). • Cars, vehicles, household goods, jewelry, other personal property (basis changes to fair market value at death). • Roth IRA held more than five tax years. • Payment from a probate estate of a sum of money or other property specifically described in a will.

These tax rules for inherited property apply to property acquired from a decedent, including assets that pass through probate, assets in a decedent's revocable trust, and assets inherited directly by joint tenants and designated beneficiaries. These rules do not apply if a gift of the asset was completed before death.

45

HAPPY & SECURE IN SONOMA COUNTY

Key Takeaways

- When a spouse passes away, slow down and make decisions very carefully. Make sure you visit your estate attorney, your CPA and your financial advisor—there are things that need to be done.

- Follow the checklist provided above.

- Keep in mind the rules of taxation on inherited property.

- Get the details about my Wealth Integration Review process, and consider a broad review/evaluation of your financial situation when you are ready. See the Free Resources page at the end of the book.

- The simplest step toward financial freedom for many people—perhaps the most valuable step—may be moving from a short term financial outlook to a long term financial outlook.

46

Chapter 5

Retiring in Sonoma County vs. Somewhere Else

Sonoma County is where I've raised my children, established lifelong relationships, and where I am familiar with my surroundings. Starting over, in a different community, would be worrisome to me.

May's Story

I've never really worried that much about money over the course of my life. Even when I was a kid in the Depression era my parents were extremely frugal, so we were able to get by okay; my dad taught me and my siblings ways to save money. My mother made all of our clothes as well. In fact, I never had a store-bought dress until I graduated from grammar school and got one from the Ward's catalog—what a thrill! As a teenager I was working constantly and I continued to save pennies everywhere I could. I was lucky enough to meet and fall in love with the man of my dreams at a dance, and he was the frugal type as well. Our first three dates were washing his car, watching his nephews, and learning to shoot his rifle up in the hills—not exactly the most costly activities. After Steve and I married, we bought a ranch in the Healdsburg area where we would raise our kids and a few animals. We worked hard and continued to save and be smart about our finances, and we taught our children to do the same. Once the kids were older I went to work at a drugstore, and I still remember how shocked I was when they raised the greeting card price to 50¢!

When the time came for us to retire, we decided to follow our dreams. We sold the ranch, got an RV, and traveled across the nation, a trip that lasted 22 amazing years. In all that time we never seriously thought of settling down in any of the places we visited because we knew home was and always would be Sonoma County. The only doubts we ever had were when we came across an RV campground in Texas where the cost of living was MUCH cheaper, and they offered assisted care for when that time came. But even while we played with the idea of settling down there we knew that we would hate to live so far away from all our kids and their families in Sonoma County.

Now I live in a granny unit behind my son Monty's house, and I absolutely love being so close to my family. They're always there to help me if I have a plumbing problem, or if I need a light bulb changed, or if I lock my keys in the car! Getting help from my family with the little things helps me live as independently as possible. I can't imagine wanting to retire away from my kids, especially if it meant leaving Sonoma County! It's a great central location with the beach, the city, and the mountains all just an hour or two away. My Kaiser health plan would make it difficult to live anywhere else, but I stay gladly. Since I've lived in Sonoma County so long, when I attend funerals for old friends, those occasions turn into little reunions. I can catch up with people, and that's something I'd definitely miss out on if I'd retired elsewhere. I still live very frugally, following my dad's advice to save for a rainy day and spend wisely. My two big splurges, my little red Volkswagen and my hot tub, are both things that I really enjoy, and I do believe they're money well spent—which is what I always strive for. A couple of my kids have considered retiring to Oregon for cheaper living, but I always tell them that they better not do that while I'm still around! I love the area, but more importantly, I love my kids, and I don't know how I'd live without them here with me.

The Advisor's Perspective

Did you catch that? "May" is my mom!

I asked my mom and dad, after their 20-plus years of traveling the U.S., "Did you ever find a place, other than Sonoma County, where you now wished you had settled down and raised your family?" Dad said, "No, Sonoma County is a very beautiful place to live."

I never heard my parents speak of retiring to any place other than Sonoma County. As my mom related in her story, they did come across an RV "retirement community" while retired and traveling through Texas, and considered settling there. But in thinking through the pros and cons, they came to the conclusion that they couldn't live so far from their family. For my dad, I'm sure what was enticing about the Texas place was that it was a VERY CHEAP place to live and they offered medical assistance for the elderly. Since mom and dad grew up in the Great Depression, cheaper living arrangements were tempting.

The idea of moving away from Sonoma County often comes up in my discussions with clients. I have heard of people moving out of the area and then regretting it. They also speak of not being able to afford to move back. Unless you have major compelling reasons to move away, you should make every attempt to stay here in this wonderful county with family and friends surrounding you.

Dad died of cancer nine years ago. Of course, I've tried every way I can to help my mom be comfortable and have peace of mind. Financially, she's pretty solid. Dad was extremely frugal and formed habits of living well within his means, and this carried over to Mom as well. She lives comfortably on her pension and Social Security income. She has no debt and her estate documents are in tip top shape.

One of the things I regret not putting in place for mom is a long term care policy. I have found that a typical stay in a nursing home, or having in-home help, can easily cost $250,000 (over this period of life). That being the case, long term care is one of those instances where it makes perfect sense to shift the risk to an insurance company.

I have since discovered a fantastic way of acquiring long term care insurance, but this was after my mom turned 80, the cut-off point for being able to qualify for it. More about this below, in the Making it Happen section.

One thing I did help Mom do to shift risk away from her and her estate was to acquire an umbrella insurance policy. This is a liability policy you take out in addition to your homeowners and auto insurance, to provide extra protection. I want my mom to be careful and safe as she's driving her cute little red VW around the back roads of Sonoma County, but realistically, senior drivers don't have the quick reflexes and safe driving abilities they once had. California had 390 traffic fatalities involving drivers age 65 or older in a recent year. People have lost fortunes due to car accidents. As my mom would say (and probably yours would too), "An ounce of prevention is worth a pound of cure."

You can easily inquire about obtaining an umbrella policy from your home or auto insurance company. If you want a good, local agent to talk to, I suggest you call Lawrence Lehr who has been helpful to me for many years. He is the owner of an Allstate Insurance agency. You will find him listed in the Resource Directory in the back of this book.

Making it Happen

I'm glad my mom and dad didn't move away after retirement. Folks in their generation typically stayed put, lived in the same house and worked for the same company until retirement.

Marketing research shows that 45 percent of American baby boomers plan to move after retirement. Most, however, want to stay close, perhaps within fifty miles or less of their former homes. Whether retirees want to stay within their home state, or move to another one, living around people their age, possibly in a planned retirement community that combines the comforts of the suburbs with the benefits of a resort, is important.

Where is the Best Place to Retire?

Oh, that's an easy one. Sonoma County! Seriously, it takes no stretch of the imagination to see the beauty and benefit of living in Sonoma County. We have the ocean, the mountains, the vineyards, the redwood forests, the Russian River, Lake Sonoma, the Sonoma County Parks, close proximity to San Francisco, and the convenience of the Charles Schulz Airport for when we want to escape. And so much more, right?

Okay, now we have that settled. So ask yourself these questions before deciding to move away:

- How does the cost of living compare from one place to another?

- If moving to another state, would your pension be taxed there?

- What's the income tax burden in the other state?

- How about <u>other</u> taxes in that area?

- Should you buy or rent a home in the new location?

- What's the climate like?

- What about doctors, healthcare and your insurance coverage?

- Can you get a decent part-time job there if you want to?

- How far will you be from your family?

- Are you sure you can move away from *This Chosen Spot of All the Earth*?

If you're still thinking of moving, where might you go?
Forbes does an annual study to determine the top 25 U.S. cities for retirement. They look at data on housing and living costs, taxes, weather and air quality, crime rates, doctor

availability, and active-lifestyle rankings for walkability, bicycling and volunteering. For 2014, here are the top cities in alphabetical order: Abilene, TX; Auburn, AL, Austin, TX; Bellingham, WA; Blacksburg, VA; Bluffton, SC; Boise, ID; Bowling Green, KY; Brevard, NC; Cape Coral, FL; Charleston, SC; Clemson, SC; Fargo, ND; Fredericksburg, TX; Las Cruces, NM; Morgantown, WV; Ogden, UT; Oklahoma City, OK; Pittsburgh, PA; Port Saint Lucie, FL; Salt Lake City, UT; San Angelo, TX; State College, PA; Tucson, AZ; and Venice, FL. I notice Bedford Falls, NY didn't make the list. Must be Henry Potter's fault. Yep—just me teasing.

AARP puts out their own list of 10 low-cost cities where you can live in comfort no matter how big (or small) your savings account. You can access this list easily on the internet.

International Living Magazine puts out a list of best places to retire overseas. They say you can retire to a place with warmer weather, a better quality of life, less crime, more cultural activities, healthier and less expensive food, better and less-expensive health care . . . and you can do it for $2,000 a month or less. However, watch out for the sales hype. Retirement promoters offer deals in supposedly friendly, low-cost and exotic locations such as Mexico, Belize, Nicaragua, Costa Rica, Panama, Colombia, and Ecuador, to name just a few. Pitches to retirees for a better retirement choice often fail to mention any of the potential downsides. Make sure you consider your own personal safety, the availability of medical services, language barrier issues, homesickness (a BIG one), and unforeseen (and undisclosed!) expenses.

How about retiring onboard a ship with **Residential Ocean Liners**? Here is what their brochure says: "As a connoisseur of life, experience the exquisite expression of extravagance, with the expectation of extreme excellence, aboard a technology advanced, twin hull, luxury Residential Ocean Liner, the world's most luxurious." Ocean liner homes start at about $700,000 and go up into the $10 million range. I also read about the development of the world's largest inland passenger boat, where you can buy a condo for about $300,000 and travel America's rivers with the other 399 residents.

Income Tax Planning — Move to a No-Tax State

 State income taxes vary greatly, from a top rate of 13.3% in California (go figure!) to zero percent in Alaska. Currently, the states of Alaska, Florida, Nevada, South Dakota, Texas, Washington, and Wyoming do not have individual state income taxes. Generally, a person's choice of where to live has very little to do with state income tax rates. Proximity to family members, the weather, and employment opportunities may have a stronger influence on a person's choice of residence than state tax brackets. However, as family members move away and a taxpayer approaches the age of retirement, the desire to move to a no-tax state can become stronger.

Taxpayers who are retired and earn taxable income from investments and retirement distributions should consider moving to a no-tax state. For example, if you are receiving a pension income from California and you move to Nevada, you will avoid the state income tax. Of course, there are volumes of tax laws regarding this issue and your planning must conform to these laws or your plan may be in vain.

But, alas, there is no place like Sonoma County! So maybe you'll just have to put up with California's income tax.

Long Term Care Insurance

 What I would have purchased for my mom, but didn't know about until after she turned 80, was an asset-based long term care insurance policy. This is a policy which is purchased with a one-time, lump sum premium payment. The beauty here is that it locks in your benefits and you never have to worry about receiving notice of a premium increase. I've had clients who owned policies on which they paid monthly premiums which eventually became unaffordable—to the point where they had to cancel the policy.

So you can see how asset-based LTC policies work, here are the numbers from an insurance proposal I recently ran and recommended to a client. This client is a single woman, age 59, retired and financially secure. If she were to deposit $100,000 into this policy:

- She would receive $586,926 in long term care benefits.

- This policy would pay out $8,151.75 per month for six years, once she was eligible for the benefit.

- Assuming she died without ever needing the LTC benefit, it would convert to a tax-free death benefit payable to her heirs in the amount of $265,164.

- Another nice feature of this policy is that should she want to, she can cancel the policy and receive a full refund of her $100,000 premium.

Under the policy I recommend, you become eligible for benefits when you can no longer perform two Activities of Daily Living (ADLs). ADLs are defined as "the things we normally do...such as feeding ourselves, bathing, dressing, grooming, work, homemaking, and leisure." Other policies may work differently.

Helping Aging Parents

 While this isn't an issue with my mom, this seems like a good place to interject this topic . . . helping our parents who have debilitating ailments and disease.

Every eighth American aged 65 and older has Alzheimer's disease, and 43% of Americans aged 85 and older have it, according to the Alzheimer's Association. Consider those percentages in light of the Social Security Administration's estimate that about 25% of today's 65-year-olds will live past age 90. These shocking statistics have serious implications for family wealth.

What are your options when it comes to helping a parent out with money management? Informally, you can "lend a helping hand" and check in with Mom and Dad to make sure that bills and premiums are paid, and deadlines are met. But if you elect to formally take the financial reins, you are looking at a two-phase process:

1. *You can get a power of attorney and assume some of the financial responsibilities.* A power of attorney is a detailed and strictly constructed legal document that gives you explicitly stated measures of financial authority. If you try to handle financial matters for your parent(s) without a valid power of attorney, financial institutions involved may reject your efforts.

A *durable* power of attorney lets you handle the financial matters of another person immediately upon signing. The alternative— a *springing* power of attorney—only takes effect when a medical diagnosis confirms that person's mental incompetence. Copies of the power of attorney should be sent to any financial institution at which your parents have accounts or policies. It may be wise to get a durable power of attorney *before* your parent is unable to make financial decisions; many investment firms require the original account owner to sign a form to allow another party access to an account owner's invested assets.

You'll need to hunt down the answers to these questions:

- What are your mom or dad's income sources (SSI, pensions, investments, etc.)?

- Where are the wills, deeds and trust documents located?

- Who are the designated beneficiaries on insurance policies, IRAs, etc.?

- Who are the members of your mom or dad's financial team or circle? You need to talk with them; they need to talk with you.

- Do you know the crucial numbers: checking and savings accounts, investment accounts, insurance policies, PINs and of course Social Security numbers?

- What is their medical history, who are their doctors, and what prescriptions do they have?

If their disease or disability progresses to the point where your mom or dad can't make competent financial decisions, then you are looking at a conservatorship. In that case...

2. You can act to become your mom or dad's conservator. This means going to probate court. You or your parent can initiate a request for conservatorship with a family law attorney; if the need is more immediate, you or your family's attorney may petition the court. In either case, you will need to show documentation that your parent is no longer financially competent. You must provide medical documentation of his or her dementia or incapacity to the court as well.

The court will interview the involved parties, look at the documentation and perform a background check on the proposed conservator. This is all pursuant to a hearing at which the court presents its decision. If conservatorship is granted, the conservator assumes control of some or all of the protected party's income and assets.

How do conservatorships differ from guardianships? A guardianship gives a guardian control over many aspects of a protected person's life. A conservatorship limits control to the management of the protected person's assets and financial affairs.

What if you don't want to assume this kind of responsibility? Some wealth management firms offer daily money management as an option in a "family office" suite of services. The firms make home visits to help with bill paying, filing medical claims and other recurring tasks. Carefully scrutinize anyone offering this service. The other choice is to give a relative, a financial services professional, or a family lawyer durable or springing power of attorney or limited or full conservatorship. Such a decision must not be made lightly. Paid caregivers generally should NOT handle financial matters.

Keep your parents away from unprincipled people. The above steps may prove essential, yet they will not shield your family from scam artists. Be on the lookout for new friends and acquaintances. If your instincts tell you something is wrong, investigate.

Key Takeaways

- Homesickness is a big issue for people moving after retirement. Don't make an irreversible move. Test the waters first, and ask yourself the questions about moving away listed in this chapter.

- State income tax rates are just one consideration of where to live in retirement. Study them carefully and don't let tax rates be the driving factor.

- For your senior parent who is still driving, shift risk from his or her estate by acquiring an umbrella insurance policy.

- Age 80 is the cut-off point for being able to buy long term care insurance, so don't put it off. The older you are, the more expensive it is.

- Consider your options and be aware of the information that will be needed when it comes to helping a parent with money management issues as they age.

Chapter 6

Make Your Heirs Really Happy

My retirement was looking pretty dismal until my generous neighbor wrote me into his will. This was all wonderful, until I realized at his passing that his estate documents weren't the best and other potential beneficiaries were starting to make waves.

Frances's Story

I grew into young adulthood during what now seems like an idyllic time in American culture—the mid 40s, 50s and 60s—in what was then considered a traditional American household. My mother and father remained together for 63 years, until my father's death. My mother is now 92, healthy and still living independently—largely because of her financial prudence—in the home my parents designed and had built in Southern California. My mother was a stay-at-home mom; my father was the breadwinner. Both my parents were honest and hardworking, and they taught their children these traits through example. My parents did not incur debt. These were not the days of living off credit cards and mindlessly shopping online or on TV. Heck—we didn't even have television until I was 10!

But in spite of this excellent example, I couldn't spend my allowance or babysitting money fast enough. (I earned $.35 to $.50 an hour back then!) These frivolous spending habits remained throughout my adult years as well. I always worked hard and paid my rent and bills on time, but what remained got spent. I confess that I was boneheaded about money and seemed to live in a magical dream world where the future was so intangible that I didn't need to plan for my retirement. I had good jobs with excellent companies, and I should have been socking away every dime I could. But my life as a collector—an acquirer of "things"—wasn't plumping up my nonexistent 401(k). I didn't make a single wise financial decision.

Fast forward to 2000, when I moved to Sonoma County and rented a granny unit. One day my landlord invited me and our next door neighbor over for homemade apple pie. Our neighbor, Ollie, was an older retired gentleman. He was a lifelong bachelor and an only child. He lived simply and was a frugal man who'd lived in the same place since he was 16, and he was now nearing 80. We had a nice, neighborly visit, and from time to time he and I engaged in lively conversations over the fence.

One day Ollie asked if I could drive him to his doctor, as a condition in his legs had worsened. I took him to the doctor, and the end result was that his legs required cleaning, an application of medication and wrapping twice a day. Guess who was appointed the caregiver for Ollie's in-home treatment?

This turned out to be less of a chore and more a time of bonding and getting to know this quirky, interesting man. I would clean and medicate his legs, and then we would sit back and talk for hours. Over time, I assisted him more, especially when he was no longer able to drive.

Ollie became my best friend, and he often told me I was his. Eventually he asked me to become the executor of his estate. He also wanted to bequeath me his home and some other assets. For a lot of reasons this was a tricky endeavor, as it required important changes to an existing trust and altering or dashing the expectations of others. Ollie knew what he wanted, but it took a while for him to fully grasp the legalities involved and implement the changes.

When Ollie died at age 87 I immediately began the task of administering his trust. It became more challenging than it should have been when I discovered that the prospect of inheritance brought out the worst in some people. People I thought I knew and trusted became demanding, self-serving, dishonest and greedy. Eventually everything was settled, but I was disheartened. I'd learned some hard life lessons along the way, and came away from this experience with an even firmer belief than before that money should *never* compromise a person's integrity.

The saddest thing of all is that I was so busy with all the legal details that I never really had a chance to grieve over my good friend Ollie's death.

Because of the fluke of having Ollie as my neighbor, and because of the generosity of this special man, I had enough of an inheritance to comfortably retire soon after his death. I already knew I wanted to open an investment account with Monty, whom I knew and trusted. I've discovered that money can bring a sense of peace and a certain independence. But I was fortunate. Not everyone who spends unwisely and doesn't plan for their future can count on a gift like this! I have friends my age who have not planned for retirement, and they face the daunting prospect of working indefinitely.

My most important financial lesson: Plan now, and plan well. Most important life lessons: Ah—that's a story for another day . . .

The Advisor's Perspective

I had been managing a small amount of money for Frances for a number of years prior to this estate matter erupting. She had unfulfilled dreams and aspirations for the future, but very little money in the bank and not much of a retirement account. She didn't even own her house. She was still working at age 62 and had no hopes of a retirement date in sight.

She brought Ollie to me for financial help a couple of years prior to his passing. I took over the management of an investment account of his and prepared his income tax returns. I also advised him to have his estate documents reviewed and updated if necessary.

For whatever reason, Ollie resisted change when it came to his estate plan. He owned two pieces of real estate, potentially valued at several million dollars or more. At the time, the estate tax exemption amount was two million, so there was a good chance that a significant amount of estate tax would be due to the IRS. We discussed several different scenarios, with various valuations of his real estate, and the possibility of his estate owing the IRS hundreds of thousands of dollars, up to perhaps a million dollars.

I gave Ollie some estate planning suggestions to minimize the tax. I think his resistance was related to the fees involved in having his real estate appraised and paying an attorney to update his estate documents. I'm sure all of this would have cost less than $10,000—a small amount in comparison to the potential tax savings, but a huge amount to this very frugal gentleman.

Fortunately, depending on how you look at it, his estate's value came in just under the $2 million exemption amount when he passed away. No estate tax was due, but this is where the real nightmare began.

Frances found that being the executor of someone's estate, while seemingly an honor, is no cake walk. Ollie's friends and neighbors, the other heirs of his estate, all came out to do battle. They were all looking for ways to increase their share and minimize that of the other heirs.

Ollie surely never imagined what drama and heartache would follow the kind words and polite smiles of the heirs at his funeral. Had he known, I'm sure he would have been more careful in drafting his estate documents, keeping them current and even being more transparent to his heirs about his intentions.

Since Ollie had no children or close family to leave his estate to, he was leaving it to his friends. The problem was, his list of friends grew over time and the new friends didn't know about the old friends. Some thought they were inheriting a much larger share than what it turned out to be. Ollie put Frances, his executor, in a very difficult position.

Fortunately, Frances is a real sweetheart of a lady. I remember listening to her as she updated me on the settling of the estate and I marveled at her diplomacy and tact in dealing with her co-heirs. She was fair and honest and didn't stoop to their level, qualities I can't help but appreciate. It made me want to help her all the more.

Now, let me share some thoughts with you which will help remove these executor challenges for the Frances in your life. Getting your estate in order and having four essential estate documents created and kept current is a real gift to your heirs. Show your love; get your estate in order.

Making it Happen

I'm not an estate attorney, so I don't draft legal documents or go too far into the legal issues of complex estate issues. My experience comes from many, many years of working on income tax and estate tax matters. As a wealth manager who has been involved in settling numerous estates, I want to let you know about some sticky issues, the documents you should have and why you should have them.

Choosing an Executor

 While beneficiaries don't need any special skills to qualify for inclusion in your will, executors do. The job of collecting your assets, paying your bills, and resolving legal and tax issues can be complicated and time consuming. That means you should ask the consent of the person you want to fill the executor's role. You should also name an alternative executor, should your first choice be unable or unwilling to do the job when the time comes, or the choice will be left to the probate court.

A spouse, child, or close friend (Frances) is frequently named executor, and can handle the task if he or she is comfortable managing legal and financial issues. It's an added advantage if he or she can work with a family lawyer. With complex estates, however, or wills which might provoke controversy, it's often best to name an executor with professional skills. One solution may be to name joint executors, such as a lawyer and a family member or friend. Had Ollie done this, Frances could have escaped the settling of his estate unscathed and perhaps even maintained friendly relations with the other heirs.

Conflicts of Interest

If you want your will to resolve—not create—controversy over your estate, you should consider potential conflicts of interest in naming your executor. Ollie didn't think this through as carefully as he should have, and as carefully as you should.

Problems arise most often when the executor's responsibility to act in the best interests of the beneficiaries competes with his or her own best interest. For example, if your executor was your business partner and your will specified that the business should buy out your share, how would the executor set the price? Would the goal be to add the most value to your estate or pay the lowest price the business could get away with?

Similarly, you might create bad feelings, or even spark a contest to your will, by naming one of your children as both executor and primary beneficiary of your estate. Though the conversation could be a painful one, many experts advise explaining the contents of your will to your family while you are able. That step could prevent conflict after you die.

Now, let's review the four essential estate planning documents you will most likely need: the will, the trust, the power of attorney, and the advance healthcare directive.

The Will

A will is a legal document that transfers your property after you die, and names the various people who will settle your estate, care for your minor children, and administer any trusts the will establishes. With rare exceptions, a will has to be a formal, written document that meets the legal requirements of the state where it's executed, or prepared. In some circumstances, a hand-written will, known as a holographic will, passes muster. In very rare cases—usually a deathbed situation—an oral will, known as a nuncupative will, may be considered valid. But why take a chance?

Making a will is one situation where doing the right thing is easy and relatively inexpensive.

The Trust

 Like a will, a trust is a written document that transfers property. But while a will is a statement of what you want to happen to your personal possessions after you die, a trust is a multipurpose tool that you can establish at any time to manage your property, distribute assets to your beneficiaries, avoid probate and save on taxes.

Since a single trust might not accomplish everything you may want to achieve, you can establish different trusts to serve different functions or benefit different people or organizations. Restrictions on trusts vary. To reduce your taxes, for example, you have to put your property into a permanent and unchangeable trust. But trusts you establish solely to manage your assets can be changed as your circumstances change.

There are many different types of trusts. The most common is referred to as a family trust or living trust. A living trust is set up while you're alive. You can serve as the trustee yourself—though you usually name someone to succeed you when you die or if you're unable to serve. Its primary goals are asset management and transferring property outside the probate process. There may or may not be tax advantages.

The Power of Attorney

 Being a property owner gives you the right to control what happens to that property, at least as long as you are healthy, solvent, and of sound mind. And, of course, it also helps if you're around to keep your eye on it. But what happens if you aren't able to exercise control for one reason or another? (Such as being out of town for an extended period or out of the country.)

One solution is to grant power of attorney to your spouse, sibling, adult child, or close friend—someone you trust to act wisely and in your best interests. This attorney-in-fact, or agent, has the legal right to make the decisions you would make if you were able, as well as the authority to buy and sell property and to write checks on your accounts.

A lawyer can draw up the power of attorney for you, specifying the authority you are granting, and excluding those things you still want to control. Many experts suggest that you, as grantor, or principal, update a power of attorney—or even write a new one— every four or five years so it will be less vulnerable to legal challenges.

Since an ordinary power of attorney is revoked if you become physically or mentally disabled, you can take the additional step of granting durable power of attorney. Unlike a limited or ordinary agreement, durable power is not revoked if you become incompetent, so you're not left without someone to act for you when you need assistance most. But not all states allow durable power, so check with your legal advisor.

The Advance Healthcare Directive

 An advance healthcare directive is a legal document in which a person specifies what actions should be taken for their health if they are no longer able to make decisions for themselves because of illness or incapacity.

Advance directives were created in response to the increasing sophistication and prevalence of medical technology. Of U.S. deaths, 25%-55% occur in health care facilities. Numerous studies have documented critical deficits in the medical care of the dying; it has been found to be unnecessarily prolonged, painful, expensive, and emotionally burdensome to both patients and their families. That should help motivate you to get this document—pronto.

Finding an Attorney Who Can Prepare Your Estate Documents

Having these four estate documents is critical. But now that you are aware of them, don't march right out and set up these documents with the first lawyer you see! It is important that you choose a lawyer who knows and understands their use, especially in your personal situation. I have heard many horror stories of people who sought help from an attorney to draft the documents, and even paid a lot of money for it, only to discover that the trust had not been funded properly, or the provisions did not reflect their wishes.

Below are some attorney-shopping guidelines to help you avoid mistakes which your heirs will have to pay for later.

You should look for an expert who creates estate documents and does estate planning exclusively, and has worked in this field for at least five years.

Ask for references.

I don't know why people have such a hard time asking professionals for references, whether a doctor, lawyer, or stockbroker, but you should ask for them and make the phone calls. Ask the attorney's clients about the service they received. How much time was spent with them? Were the documents explained in detail? Did the attorney answer their questions?

Find out exactly what the fees and services will be.

Get this information up front. I suggest you find an attorney who provides you with a flat-fee quote. This way, if the attorney misjudges what it costs to create your documents, he or she is obliged to complete the work, but it shouldn't cost you more.

You want to make sure your attorney will be funding the trust for you. This is done by changing the title of your assets from your name to the trust's name. The fee you pay a lawyer should include making the necessary document changes for you. It will do you absolutely no good to have trust documents drawn up if your assets are not put into the trust.

Remember, you get what you pay for. Stay away from "trust mills," which are lawyers who come into town, host a trust seminar, take your money and then leave town. Sure, you get your "binder" of documents in the mail, but are they correct? For similar reasons, online internet sites are equally scary.

The lawyer you select should also be able to advise you on estate planning.

This seems so obvious, but if the lawyer you're working with does not specialize in this field, the value to you is diminished. A lawyer should look out for your best interests in a number of ways. Subjects such as beneficiary designations, long term care insurance, an advance healthcare directive, gifting programs, and your charitable inclinations should come up. Look for this type of expanded and detailed service. For example, what would be the point of setting up a trust only to see your assets dwindle from long term care costs? Remember, a revocable trust does not protect your assets. It only bypasses probate.

Does the lawyer you're considering actually listen to you?

When you visit the office, pay close attention to who is doing all the talking. Hint: it should be you. The lawyer should be asking you questions and then carefully listening to you. What is it that you want? What is important to you? Why? What don't you want? Etc., etc. Every professional you hire should be a good listener.

You Can Be The Millionaire Next Door

 Ollie was one of the millionaire next door types written about by Thomas Stanley in his book, *The Millionaire Next Door*. (See reference in the Resources section at the end of the book.) No one would have known of his accumulated wealth by observing him and his modest home. Frances, on the other hand, didn't have the millionaire mindset as she admitted to being more of a spender. But she could have been one! The millionaire next door is not a men's club.

From the Introduction to *The Millionaire Next Door*:

> "We have discovered who the wealthy really are and who they are not. And, most important, we have determined how ordinary people can become wealthy.
>
> What is so profound about these discoveries? Just this: Most people have it all wrong about wealth in America. Wealth is not the same as income. If you make a good income each year and spend it all, you are not getting wealthier. You are just living high. Wealth is what you accumulate, not what you spend.
>
> How do you become wealthy? Here, too, most people have it wrong. It is seldom luck or inheritance or advanced degrees or even intelligence that enables people to amass fortunes. Wealth is more often the result of a lifestyle of hard work, perseverance, planning, and most of all, self-discipline."

Ollie had a couple things in common with the millionaire next door types: he lived well below his means, and he believed that financial independence was more important than displaying high social status. He had a lifestyle conducive to accumulating money.

Meanwhile, Frances was one of those who lived pretty much paycheck to paycheck. Don't get me wrong, she's a fine, decent person, and honest as the day is long. She pays her bills, and she doesn't go into debt . . . or date men who do. However, accumulation of wealth or becoming financially independent were not on her radar, or perhaps were postponed decade after decade, with the idea that she had plenty of time for such matters.

My experience tells me that most people approach household financial decisions as short term decisions. They are geared toward this month or this year, and often relate to cash flow management or debt management. The simplest step toward financial freedom—perhaps the most valuable step—may be moving from a short term financial outlook to a long term financial outlook.

Think about becoming the "millionaire next door." In many cases in this country, wealth is grown slowly and steadily. We all dream of a windfall, but usually individuals amass $1 million or more through a variety of factors: ongoing investment according to a consistent financial strategy, the compounding of assets/savings over time, business or professional success, and perhaps even inherited wealth.

When the focus moves from "How do we make it work this month?" to "How do we make moves in pursuit of our financial goals?" the whole outlook on the meaning and purpose of money begins to change. What should money do for you? What purpose should it have in your life? What can you do to make it work harder for you, so that you might not have to work as hard in the future?

You have the wisdom, prudence and patience to be a superb investor. Understanding the financial world is ultimately a matter of learning its "language" and precepts, which will quickly seem less arcane with education. Today, do yourself a money favor and talk with a financial professional who can help you define long term and lifetime financial goals and direct some of your money in pursuit of them.

Income Tax Planning — Medi-Cal Eligibility and Capital Gains

 Ollie didn't make large gifts of his assets while he was living. Many people do, however, and should think twice before doing so. Gifts can affect eligibility for Medi-Cal benefits for nursing home care. (Medi-Cal is California's Medicaid program.) Giving an asset during life rather than allowing it to pass at death can create capital gains taxes.

Those who may require Medi-Cal, particularly married couples, should consult a lawyer before making substantial gifts. Medi-Cal rules include protections for a person whose spouse requires nursing home care. Gifts can interfere with those protections. If you're thinking of giving a capital asset, it's wise to compare the basis rules for gifts and inherited assets before deciding on the gift.

These examples will help you see the impact of gifting:

Example #1: Debbie transferred title of her house to her two daughters 15 years ago. At the time of the gift, Debbie's basis was

$50,000 and the value of the house was $250,000. Debbie, a widow, continued to live alone in the house and pay all the bills as if she still owned it. Debbie moved into a memory care facility earlier this year after she was diagnosed with Alzheimer's disease. She depleted her savings and is now receiving state assistance. Because the gift of her house was made long before she needed assistance, Debbie was not disqualified from receiving benefits. Debbie's daughters sold her house for $550,000. Because they received the house as a gift, they take Debbie's basis of $50,000 and have a taxable capital gain of $500,000. Although Debbie's daughters will pay capital gains tax, they received an asset that would likely have been used to pay Debbie's medical bills.

Example #2: Assume the same facts as Example #1, except that Debbie tries to outsmart the folks at the Medi-Cal office by transferring title of her house to her two daughters three months prior to moving to the memory care facility. She does this, perhaps with someone's coaching, in an attempt to qualify for Medi-Cal and keep her house out of the picture. Owning a house at the time she applies for Medi-Cal is not a problem. The problem appears when Debbie dies and the Medi-Cal office sends the estate a bill for all the services paid for by Medi-Cal—this is called *estate recovery*.

California uses a 60-month look-back penalty period for gifting or transferring assets to create eligibility for Medi-Cal benefits. No gifts are safe until five years pass from the date of the gift to the date of application for Medi-Cal. Therefore, Debbie's gift to her daughters, just three months prior, will be disallowed and the house pulled back into the estate. The house will have to be sold and the Medi-Cal bill paid.

Example #3: Now let's say that Debbie has not given her house to her daughters and her health is excellent, at least until she is hit by a bus and killed instantly. The basis of Debbie's house would step up to the date of death value of $550,000. Her daughters would inherit the house, and have had no capital gain and no tax to pay.

Key Takeaways

- The job of collecting your assets, paying your bills, and resolving legal and tax issues after your death can be complicated and time consuming. Choose your executor and successor trustee carefully.

- Getting your estate in order and having the four essential estate documents created and kept current is a real gift to your heirs. Show your love; get your estate in order.

- If you want help clarifying instructions to your heirs, you may request a copy of my Letter of Instruction Guidelines worksheet. See the Free Resources page at the end of the book.

- For further help, you may request a copy of my Advisor List & Document Locator worksheet. See the Free Resources page at the end of the book.

- Use the attorney-shopping guidelines above to help avoid mistakes your family cannot afford.

- Giving away your property or making cash gifts can affect eligibility for Medi-Cal benefits for nursing home care. Think twice about gifting, and consider the tax consequences, too.

Chapter 7

Choosing the Right Advisor

I did everything right in terms of saving and preparing for retirement. What wiped me out was trusting the wrong advisor.

Sharon's Story

After my divorce in 1977, I moved from San Francisco to Sonoma County with my two daughters. At first it was really hard; my job only paid $4.90 an hour, and I had sizable house payments to worry about. When I got my first raise (to $5.10 an hour), I started putting the maximum percentage of my paycheck into the company's employee stock ownership plan. Financial security was a top priority for me, and I was determined to start saving early for retirement. I managed to rise through the ranks of the company and survive several rounds of layoffs over the years. Since I had risen to a management position and had long been reserving the maximum percentage of my pay for the stock ownership plan as well as saving pennies in everyday life, I managed to retire at age 58 with good stock options and $1.5 million. Even with some classes on financial planning under my belt, I didn't feel confident managing all that money by myself, so I decided to find someone who could manage it for me.

I went to a nationally known brokerage house and put full trust in my advisor, thinking that having fancy initials after your name meant having experience and expertise. In reality, my advisor was extremely incompetent, and my nest egg dropped from $1.5 million to $860,000 in two years because he kept my money in badly chosen stocks. He was only focused on buying and selling stocks with my money, and he didn't pay attention to what I needed: a reliable income for retirement. He kept assuring me that the money I lost in stocks would come right back, but it never did, and his fees were whittling away my income. To top it all off, he didn't consider the major tax consequences of exercising the stock options from my employer, and I was then forced to sell all those shares to pay the taxes. At that point, I decided to leave the brokerage house and take some classes on investments so I could make a better choice the next time around. But every potential advisor I talked to seemed the same as the first guy: money-grubbing, inexperienced, and uninterested in my needs. That's when a friend referred me to Jerry.

My first meeting with Jerry made me feel hopeful that he could save the rest of my retirement money: He had even more fancy initials than the rest, and he talked a lot about investing in property rather than in stocks, which sounded like a more stable strategy. He promised me enough income to live on every month, which was most important to me at that point. I signed on with him at that meeting, and everything seemed to be going fine for a while. He was very confident that I would no longer have to worry about losing money, and that healthcare real estate would be an important investment as the population aged. I had no reservations about letting him manage all my remaining funds. He also suggested that I refinance my home for some more cash, and that move enabled me to make some improvements that made my home more valuable. But that turned out to be the only good thing to come out of working with Jerry.

Red flags started appearing about five years after I became his client. The first sign that things were going awry was that I started missing some of my monthly income payments. When I asked Jerry about it, he told me not to worry; he said that he'd just sell one of the properties and give me the funds from that. But that money never materialized. The tax preparer I was using, recommended by Jerry, commented that the property investments I had were riskier than Jerry made them out to be, but Jerry just got mad when I asked about it and said that the tax preparer had no idea what he was talking about. I found pretty big errors on forms Jerry had filled out and pressured me to sign, but my requests for corrected copies were brushed aside. I started getting really suspicious, and then I spotted an article in the newspaper reporting that Jerry was closing his doors and being investigated for fraud, and that his partner had already served time in federal prison for fraud. I never heard from Jerry again, but I did hear from some of Jerry's other clients as we tried to figure out what was going on. Jerry was later found guilty of fraud and sent to prison, leaving myself and hundreds of others with hundreds of thousands of dollars lost. Jerry had only diversified with a small sum in another company, so I had only $200,000 of my original $1.5 million left to my name. I could only think, "How am I possibly going to live for the rest of my life on that amount?" I had to start saving pennies again, but worse than my own inconvenience was the fact that I could no longer help my daughters with their college expenses. I was so proud of them for being the first in my family to get degrees, and I had looked forward to helping them pay off their loans, but that was no longer a possibility.

My advice to people searching for financial advisors? Self-educate. In my day, women weren't expected to learn anything about financial planning, and this made it really difficult for me to find a good advisor and really understand what he was doing with my money. Make sure that your advisor is not just confident and loaded with fancy initials, but is also experienced and more interested in your needs than his own. Be assertive with your questions and your needs, and pay attention to those little red flags. Being an introvert myself, I know how difficult it is to really assert yourself to these confident money-men, but I think it's a really important thing to do for a strong and effective client-advisor relationship.

The Advisor's Perspective

Sharon did everything right in building for a secure retirement. She started saving early and kept increasing her savings rate as she earned pay raises. She amassed a fine nest egg of $1.5 million and retired in 2000, believing she was safe and secure. Sharon was the millionaire next door! She definitely deserves a gold star for her vocational achievements and overcoming the many financial struggles she started out with. She's a real sweet lady too!

Upon retirement, Sharon rolled over her nest egg to the big boys at the largest brokerage house in the world. Unfortunately, she was put with a financial advisor who didn't listen to her, didn't protect her and ultimately lost $600,000 of her nest egg during the 2000-2002 "tech bubble" market crash. I have seen this too many times when people place their trust in the national brand big brick and mortar establishments. Please believe me, it's not the company that is important, it's the individual advisor you work with. You want someone you can sit down with face-to-face, look in the eye and develop a trusted long term relationship with.

In 2002 Sharon moved to another advisor, who I'll call Jerry, with an independent firm in Santa Rosa. Jerry was referred to her by a friend. He was a confident and persuasive individual. Jerry convinced Sharon to put most all of her money into various real estate partnerships. What I don't think she realized was that these investments were not liquid or marketable, making it very difficult to understand their true value or to pull out if needed. Jerry defrauded her and many others in Sonoma County out of approximately $200 million. Jerry is now in prison.

In 2008, Sharon was referred to me by one of my widowed clients. I helped Sharon transfer her accounts away from Jerry and protect what she had left. She got out with only about $200,000 remaining of her nest egg. I would have loved to have been the judge who got to send Jerry to prison.

Sharon's retirement has had a very rough beginning—one incompetent advisor and one dishonest advisor. Now, I guess I'm the "clean-up" guy and I've been helping her for the last five years. I'm doing everything I can to put a smile back on her face. Things have stabilized. However, considering that 87% of her nest egg went up in smoke and she is now in her 70s, her ability to support herself is a real issue.

It has been my job to help Sharon recover and move on. I ran a retirement projection to get a picture of what her cash flow would look like going forward. As expected, the projection indicated that she was going to need to take some pretty drastic action to maintain some security. One of the ideas we discussed was getting a reverse mortgage on her house. She was dead set against it initially, but some years later she came to realize that doing a reverse mortgage would be very beneficial.

We've explored lots of options, like selling her house and buying a mobile home or renting an apartment. We also talked about her taking in a tenant or moving in with one of her kids. These are tough choices she never thought she would be facing. It is difficult to make these decisions, holding back the tears while looking at your retirement projection which says you're going to run out of money before you turn 80.

Ultimately, the decision was made to take out a reverse mortgage on her house. Of course it's not ideal, but in her case it can really help her out. The reverse mortgage has allowed her to stop making a mortgage payment and therefore reduce the monthly withdrawal on her dwindling IRA. I'll talk more about the reverse mortgage in the Making it Happen section.

Making it Happen

You need help with your investments. But how do you find the right advisor for your needs and goals?

- Where do you start?
- Which advisor is right for you?
- How do you know you are asking the right questions?

Guidelines for Avoiding the "Evil Advisor"

Here are some simple guidelines to help you avoid getting the "evil advisor." Sharon would probably suggest you pay close attention here!

Selecting an investment advisor can be a daunting task. Getting answers to the following seven questions will improve your chances of success.

1. How "hands on" do you want to be in managing your investments?

The most important question you can ask is one you ask yourself: "What do I want and how do I want to accomplish it?" As Dr. Steven Covey, the author of *The Seven Habits of Highly Effective People* said, "Put first things first."

- Do you want to manage your own investments on a day-to-day basis?

- Do you only want advice on how to manage your investments?

- Or do you want to hire a skilled manager to direct your investments for you?

These are important questions with different implications, requiring clear but distinctive answers. For example, if you determine you would like advice on how to manage your investments, then you need to be prepared to take some responsibility for your investment's performance. Advice is just an opinion or recommendation about what could or should be done. Responsibility for your investment's performance still rests squarely on your shoulders. On the other hand, if you hire a portfolio manager to manage your investments, then by definition that manager is taking ownership and responsibility for the performance of that account.

Once you are clear on what you want, you can move on to questions for the advisor . . .

2. How do you get paid?

This is the most important question you can ask a potential advisor. Why is this question so important? Because you need some assurance that your advisor is working in <u>your</u> best interest—not his or hers.

Advisors and financial planners are compensated in many different ways, but the majority of advisors either charge commissions or fees, or both.

Commissions

Commissions or sales charges come in several forms. First, you may pay a commission when the advisor buys or sells a stock, bond, or Exchange Traded Fund (ETF). You may also pay a commission when an advisor sells you a mutual fund. These charges are often called sales loads or sales fees. Commissions tend to be the best choice when you know exactly what you want, or if very few transactions are planned.

The problem with commissions or sales loads is that you pay the advisor up front. Imagine if a realtor was paid up front to sell a house. What incentive would the realtor have to ensure the house actually sells? Additionally, because the advisor may receive higher commissions for some investments than for others, commissions can often drive a product sale—which may not actually meet your goals.

Fees

There are two types of fees. First there are flat or hourly fees, similar to how attorneys or CPAs bill their clients. With hourly fees it is important to define up front which services will be performed, and to receive an estimate of the total cost.

The second type of fee is based on assets under management. This fee is usually between one and three percent of the account balance per year. This compensation method is best when you hire an advisor to manage your portfolio on an ongoing basis. When the compensation method is a fee based on assets under management, the advisor can only get a raise if he or she grows your account. But take note; some advisors base their fees on all of your assets, including your real estate, not just the securities directly under their management.

3. How will you invest my money?

It is critical that the advisor has a clear plan for investing your money.

- How will the advisor determine which investments are right for you?

- Is the plan customizable or one-size-fits-all?

- Will the plan change with your changing goals?

- How would the investments change in a deteriorating economic environment?

The answers to these questions should be clear and intelligent. Ask for clarification about how the advisor's recommendations fit your goals. (See Appendix 1 for a little about my approach to investing.)

4. Do you have an exit strategy for my portfolio?

This is where most advisors fail. Nothing goes up forever. Therefore, it is imperative to know when to take the chips off the table.

Warren Buffett once said that there are only two rules to investing. Rule #1: Don't lose money. Rule #2: Never forget Rule #1.

FUN POP QUIZ:

If your portfolio loses 25% of its value this year, what return would you need next year to break even?

Investment Year #1 Starting Value = $100,000 Return = -25% Ending Value = ?

$100,000 x (1-.25) = $75,000

Investment Year #2 Starting Value = $75,000 Return = ? Ending Value = $100,000

($100,000 - $75,000)/$75,000 = 33.3%

> Did you get the correct answer? If you lose 25% of your portfolio, it takes a 33.3% return just to break even! If you lose 50% of your money you need a 100% return just to break even! That is why it is critical not to lose money. And not to trust an advisor who says "Don't worry, we'll make it back next year."

The main reason so many investors lost money in the last down market is that they, or their advisors, did not have exit strategies. Advisors need to have predefined plans for what they will do if investments lose money. Remember, there is no reason to be emotionally attached to any investment. Investments are designed for one thing and one thing only: to make money.

 ### 5. As an advisor, are you driven to "beat the market?"

This may sound counter-intuitive; after all, who doesn't want to beat the market? However, the most successful investment portfolios are those that are principle-driven and fundamentally managed for the specific achievement of long term financial goals. The truth is you should not be chasing the maximum return possible anywhere in the universe. The result of such behavior is a roller-coaster ride and a level of stress which is unnecessary.

The principle-driven portfolio management system begins with the dictum that "performance" is not a financial goal, and that the only rational basis for the construction and management of a long term portfolio is your long term financial goals. Thus, questions like "When will the Fed start (or stop) raising rates?" and "What will the S&P 500 earn this year?" are subordinated, by several orders of magnitude, by the questions that really matter: (1) "Who is this money for?" (2) "What is this money for?" and (3) "When will this money be needed?"

These three questions will be very important—to the right kind of financial advisor. Watch and see if the advisor asks you these questions when you first meet. It's a clue!

Making sure the advisor has the right focus is critical. After all, if you are not paying to achieve your financial goals, what are you paying for?

6. What value do you offer—beyond investment management?

Sure, investment performance is important, but what else does the advisor do to help you accomplish your financial goals and desired lifestyle? For instance, is your investment planning integrated with your income tax planning? Are your assets properly positioned to protect you from lawsuits, college financial aid formulas, Medicare estate recovery liens, probate fees, excessive taxes, etc., etc.? Ultimately, these issues may be very costly if not handled properly. Make sure you are getting all the services you need!

And, as Columbo would say…"I've got one more question…"

7. Is this advisor "just right" for me?

I was recently told by one prospective client that he thought my firm was **TOO BIG** for his needs and he would choose another firm. Of course, I had to chuckle. What? Did he think we might overwhelm him with our excellent client service and many resources?

I had another prospective client tell me recently that she thought my firm was **TOO SMALL** for her needs and she would be going elsewhere. She wanted a firm that had a "brand" name and lots of employees—as some form of security and stability.

The truth is there is an overwhelming trend of clients moving away from large investment and CPA firms in recent years. People are realizing that they can get the personal attention they desire from a small "boutique" firm without giving up anything that really, truly matters. Many of us in small firms came from big firms and have years and years of experience—we just got tired of the bureaucracy. I have clients tell me all the time that our tax and investment services are better than what they experienced at one of the BIG firms.

In dealing with financial matters, you should be working with someone you trust. There are too many scams and evidences of incompetency to do otherwise. Big, small…why not go with "just right"—someone you trust.

SUMMARY:

Well formulated questions are the tools used to dissect any problem. Take time to ask tough questions of yourself and potential advisors.

<u>Ask yourself:</u>

1. What do you want and how do you want to accomplish it? Create a solid foundation by defining your goals.

2. Does this advisor feel "just right" for me?

<u>Ask the advisor:</u>

3. How do you get paid? Make sure the advisor's compensation method is aligned with your goals.

4. How will you invest my money? Ask tough questions. Expect intelligent answers.

5. Do you have an exit strategy? Make sure the advisor has a predefined plan to prevent major losses in your account.

6. Are you driven to "beat the market?" The focus must be to achieve your financial goals.

7. What else will you do to help me accomplish my financial objectives? The best advisors go way beyond investment advice and take a 'holistic' approach.

These questions should provide you with an excellent basis for hiring an advisor. Once you find the right advisor, you can work together to create results.

Income Tax Planning — Tax Deduction for Advisory Fees

 Now that we've explored finding the right advisor, you may be delighted to know that there are tax deductions available for investment advisory and financial planning fees. With each of my clients I'm always looking for ways to reduce income tax liability. Unfortunately, Sharon doesn't have the need for tax deductions beyond her standard deduction these days, but you might.

Congress did grant a tax deduction for certain investment expenses, but as with anything to do with the tax code, the devil's in the details. Not to worry though, it is not a lost cause, there are answers.

In general, the tax code allows for the deduction of some expenses incurred in the production of income. You can deduct things like: investment advisory fees, financial planning fees, account maintenance fees, subscriptions for investment newsletters and magazines, and investment or financial planning software. These are reported as itemized deductions on Schedule A, subject to the 2% of adjusted gross income limitation.

Keep in mind that in order for these costs to be tax deductible, you must pay the expenses from your own pocket (not taken from your IRA), they must be "ordinary and necessary" and the amount of the expense in relation to the income produced should be "reasonable and proximate."

Contrary to what may be advertised, the cost of attending seminars, on land or on water, is not deductible. Also, expenses incurred in the production of income through tax exempt investments (municipal bonds) are not deductible.

The Reverse Mortgage

 The Basics. If you are over age 62 and have lots of equity but limited income, a reverse mortgage may be an appealing alternative to selling your home. A reverse mortgage will allow you to borrow against the value of your home so that you can continue to live there. The loan does not have to be repaid until the home is no longer your primary residence. However, you must pay insurance premiums and real estate taxes to keep the loan in good standing.

You can apply for an insured reverse mortgage through a lender who is approved to offer Home Equity Conversion Mortgages (HECMs) backed by the Federal Housing Administration (FHA) or from a limited number of other private lenders. The amount you can borrow depends on your home's appraised value, the current interest rate, the age of the youngest borrower, and the amount of the initial mortgage insurance premium. (This is required insurance which guarantees that you will receive the expected loan advances.) In addition, FHA lenders impose caps on the amount they will lend.

While interest rates quoted on reverse mortgages can be similar to those for other mortgages, there are additional fees and charges that can make them more expensive than other types of loans. Lenders must provide a "Total Annual Loan Cost" disclosure that estimates the average annual cost as a percentage of the loan, and borrowers must be counseled by a HECM approved counselor.

Regulations enacted in 2013 to protect both borrowers and the FHA require, in some cases, a financial assessment before a loan is approved and an escrow account is opened. They also limit the amount that can be withdrawn in the first year of the loan.

The local expert on reverse mortgages I call in to assist my clients is Ron Seaman. You will find him listed in the Resource Directory in the back of this book.

Key Takeaways

- It's not the company that is important, it's the individual financial advisor you work with. You want someone you can sit down with face to face, look in the eye and develop a trusted long term relationship with. Brick and mortar, a long list of employees . . . all mean nothing! Choose an advisor you understand, you like and you trust. The size of the business doesn't matter.

- When hiring a financial advisor, don't be afraid to ask questions! This relationship is absolutely critical. You don't want to have an advisor who ends up in prison one day. Choose an advisor who is trustworthy, and with whom you keep a close relationship. Use the questions in this chapter as a guide.

- Taking out a reverse mortgage is not the first choice for anyone. But don't rule it out; it may be just the solution that is needed.

Chapter 8

Your Descendants Can Be Happy and Secure

T he first seven chapters and the client stories covered a lot of ground, but not the particular issue of passing on generational wealth. Sadly, this is one of those topics which doesn't get discussed enough. You should consider it.

You've built up a happy and secure lifestyle, and perhaps you're leaving a significant legacy for your kids; now it's time to look at how you can help THEM manage it wisely. You be the judge of how much is "significant." Perhaps you have millions; perhaps it's a more modest amount. Either way, you probably prefer that those who inherit your wealth use it towards their own happiness and security.

I have some stories to share with you about real people here in Sonoma County, but first take a quick peek at a couple of American families with BIG money.

There are many stories of family wealth lost. In the late 19th century, industrial tycoon Cornelius Vanderbilt amassed the equivalent of $100 billion in today's dollars—but when 120 of his descendants met at a family gathering in 1973, there were no millionaires among them.

Barbara Woolworth Hutton—daughter of the founder of E.F. Hutton & Company, heiress to the Woolworth's five-and-dime empire—inherited $900 million in inflation-adjusted dollars but passed away nearly penniless (her reputed net worth at death was $3,500).

Why do stories like these happen? Why, as the *Wall Street Journal* notes, does an average of 70% of family wealth erode in the hands of the next generation, and an average of 90% of it in the hands of the generation thereafter? And why, as the Family Business Institute notes, do only 3% of family businesses survive past the third generation?

Lost family wealth can be linked to economic, medical and psychological factors, or even changes in an industry or simple fate. But inherited wealth may also slip away for far less dramatic reasons.

Here are some of those less dramatic reasons for wealth slipping away:

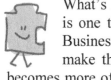
What's more valuable, money or knowledge? Having money is one thing; knowing how to make and keep it is another. Business owners naturally value control, but at times they make the mistake of valuing it too much. Being in control becomes more of a priority than sharing practical knowledge, ideas or a financial stake with the next generation. Or, maybe there simply isn't enough time in a business owner's 60-hour workweek to convey the know-how, or to set up a succession plan that makes sense for two generations. Or maybe the next generation just isn't interested in the business (like my three children, none of whom are interested in stepping into my business). A good succession planner can help a family business deal with these concerns.

Just as a long term direction is set for the family business, one should also be set for other family money. Much has been written about baby boomers being on the receiving end of the greatest generational wealth transfer in history—a total of roughly $7.6 trillion, according to the *Wall Street Journal*—but so far, young boomers are only saving about $0.50 of each $1 they inherit. If adult children grow up with a lot of money, they may also easily slip into a habit of spending beyond their means, or acting on entrepreneurial whims without the knowledge or boots-on-the-ground business acumen of Mom and Dad. According to online legal service Rocket Lawyer, 41% of baby boomers (Americans now aged 50-68) have no estate plan. Wills are a necessity, and trusts are useful as well, especially when wealth stands a chance of going to minors.

 Vision matters. When family members agree about the value and purpose of family wealth—what wealth means to them, what it should accomplish, how it should be maintained and grown for the future—that shared vision can be expressed in a coherent legacy plan, which can serve as a kind of compass.

After all, estate planning encompasses much more than strategies for wealth transfer, tax deferral and legal tax avoidance. It is also about conveying knowledge—and values. In the long run, nothing may help sustain family wealth more. I feel so strongly about the importance of passing on family values that I have offered to help my clients create a video legacy of their life, where they can share their lives and values, to be passed on to the next generation.

Six Blunders with Family Wealth

Family wealth fails to last because families fall prey to serious money blunders—old and new. Classic mistakes are made, and changing times aren't recognized.

1. Procrastination. This isn't simply a matter of failing to plan or putting off planning, it's also failing to respond to acknowledged financial weaknesses and "missing pieces."

For example, let's say we have a multimillionaire named Allen. Allen gets a call one afternoon from his bank, which considers him a VIP. It turns out that his six-figure savings account lacks a designated beneficiary. He thanks the caller, and says he will come in soon to take care of that—but he never does. His schedule is busy, and the detour is always inconvenient.

While Allen knows about this financial flaw, knowledge is one thing and action is another. Sadly, too often procrastination wins out in the end and those assets end up subject to probate. Then Allen's heirs find out about other lingering financial matters that should have been taken care of regarding his IRA, his real estate holdings, and more.

> Or consider Dorothy: A year after she created her estate plan, here in Sonoma County, she used a pencil to cross out portions of one of the original documents. She changed a provision that originally stated her house should be sold and the proceeds divided among five distant relatives. She decided, instead, to leave her home and its contents to a charitable organization. She intended, as some point, to have her attorney make these changes to the document.
>
> After her unexpected death, relatives claimed that the document was improperly altered. Two courts agreed. Thus, the original language held and the charity she cared about received nothing.

2. Minimal or absent estate planning. *Forbes* notes that 55% of Americans lack wills, and every year multimillionaires die without them—not just rock stars and actors, but also small business owners and entrepreneurs. Others opt for a living trust and a pour-over will, or just a basic will created online. This may not be enough.

Anyone reliant on a will risks handing the destiny of their wealth over to a probate judge. The multimillionaire who has a child with special needs, a family history of Alzheimer's or Parkinson's, or a former spouse or estranged children may need more rigorous estate planning. The same is true if he or she wants to endow charities or give grandkids a nice start in life. Is this person a business owner? That factor alone calls for coordinated estate and succession planning.

A finely crafted estate plan has the potential to perpetuate and enhance family wealth for decades, perhaps generations. Without it, heirs may have to deal with probate and the lost potential for tax-advantaged growth and compounding of those assets.

> Here in Sonoma County there is the story of Angelo Frati, who died in 1995 without a will or trust. His 10.5 acres on Laguna Road, just northwest of Santa Rosa, ended up in the hands of the Probate Court and were offered for sale at

auction, with the proceeds divided equally among all the heirs. It was acquired by Jim and Kathleen Dolinsek at a bargain price. Good for the Dolinseks, not so much for the Frati family. If the Frati family had any hope of maintaining their family homestead, it was lost due to the lack of estate planning.

3. The lack of a "family office." Years ago, wealthy families often chose to assign financial management to professionals. The family mansion boasted an office where those professionals worked closely with the family. While the traditional "family office" has disappeared, the concept is as relevant as ever. Today, wealth management firms consult with families, provide reports and assist in decision-making in an ongoing relationship with personal and responsive service. This is a wise choice when your financial picture becomes too complex to address on your own.

I'm aware of a family here in Sonoma County who could really benefit from the family office concept. There are eight siblings who inherited their parents' property, some 50 acres of prime agricultural property worth $1.5 million or so. At the time of inheritance, they transferred the title into their eight names, each holding a one-eighth interest as tenants in common. They met and discussed the sale of the property or other possible uses. The problem was they couldn't agree on anything. Years went by. Rather than letting it sit as raw land, they have at least agreed to grow hay and make a little money. From time to time they have family meetings to consider other options, such as growing grapes on the property. But they can't decide. How would they afford that? With the years going by, they're all getting older, and they contemplate their lost opportunity. What that money could have done for their individual families, if they could have only agreed on its use or sale! Some want out of the property, some want to keep it and develop it. No one is in a financial position to buy out any other sibling. They're in a mess. What do you think will happen when one of them dies? Perhaps this is where they could use some professional help to achieve their

> objectives. And, yes, I've suggested they do this. Problem is, they can't decide.

4. Technological flaws. Hackers can hijack email accounts and send phony messages to banks, brokerages and financial advisors greenlighting asset transfers. Social media can help you build your business, but it can also lend personal information to identity thieves who want access to digital and tangible assets.

Sometimes a business or family installs a security system that proves problematic—so much so that it is turned off half the time. Unscrupulous people have ways of learning about that. Maybe they are only one or two degrees separated from you.

5. No long term strategy in place. When a family wants to sustain wealth for decades to come, heirs have to understand the how and why. All family members have to be on the same page, or at least read that page! If family communication about wealth tends to be more opaque than transparent, the mechanics and purpose of the strategy may never be adequately conveyed to heirs.

I have some clients who are very good at family communication. Some of my senior clients will bring one of their children to an office consultation when important decisions need to be made. Others have taken me up on my offer to produce a legacy video of them telling their stories and sharing their values. This video makes a wonderful keepsake for the generations to come. These are methods of keeping long term strategies in place, or at the very least, understood.

Our firm offers to film legacy videos for our investment clients. Another option, and better, would be for you to hire a videographer to work with you directly. One I have experience with and can recommend is Kathleen Quinn of Life Reflections Video. You will see her listed in the Resource Directory in the back of this book.

6. No decision-making process. In the typical high net worth family, financial decision-making is vertical and top-down. Parents or grandparents may make a decision in private, and it may be years before heirs learn about it or fully understand it. When the heirs do become decision makers, it is usually upon the death of the elders— only now the heirs are in their forties, fifties or even sixties, with current and former spouses and perhaps children of their own to make family wealth decisions more trying.

Horizontal decision-making can help multiple generations understand and participate in the guidance of family wealth. Estate and succession planning professionals can help a family make these decisions with an awareness of different communication styles. In-depth conversations are essential; good estate planners recognize that silence does not necessarily mean agreement.

Decisions need to be made if you have any hope of keeping family wealth intact. If you have a family business, steps need to be taken to groom your successor family member(s) for the job. If it's other forms of wealth you wish to protect, there are ways to go about it. Some families will set up a family foundation or donor advised fund and appoint the children as trustees. The children oversee the use of the foundation money toward the charitable intent as laid out by the parents.

Now for some real decision-making families. Here are a few nice examples from the annual reports of the Sonoma County Community Foundation.

Soiland Family Fund. Years ago, Marv Soiland set up a donor advised fund at the Community Foundation Sonoma County. His wife and his 7 children have been a part of the fund as donors and advisors on grants to the community. Now his son, Dean and wife Belinda (Bo) have a fund for their 3 children and themselves to continue the tradition for their family. They make grants to fund important community needs in Sonoma County.

Jackson Family Fund. Barbara Banke and her late husband, Jess Jackson, have a long history of charitable giving from their trusts and foundations. They started a donor advised fund at the Community Foundation to continue the giving. Barbara Banke now plans to set up donor advised funds for each of their five children to continue the tradition of philanthropy.

Friedman Family Foundation Fund. As a result of the success of the Friedman Home Improvement Center, the Friedman Family has a long history of giving to causes in Sonoma County. They built the Friedman Center which is used by many organizations as a place for celebrations and community dinners. There are now 3 generations of family members who participate in advising on grants from their fund.

57 Point Financial Health Checklist

If you're in business for yourself, you understand the importance of customer service. Earl Nightingale gave this great advice: *"If a businessperson would just devote an hour a day to thinking of how he might be of greater service to his customers and community, he wouldn't need to give much thought to how he would pay his bills or achieve his goals."* I agree.

Customer service is extremely important to my friend Larry Dahl, owner of Oil Stop. If you have your car serviced at Oil Stop, like I do, you are familiar with their *33-Point Service Checklist*. Personally, I like the fact that they're checking on each of those 33 things each time I drop in. When I was young I blew up an engine because of the lack of ongoing professional maintenance. Recently, while I was at Oil Stop, I was thinking about this type of maintenance checklist. I thought it would be great for my clients—as it applies to *financial health,* not oil. This kind of tool could prevent you from blowing up your engine—so to speak.

I've created my own *57 Point Financial Health Checklist.* It's quite comprehensive and I'm certain it would be beneficial for you. See the Free Resources page at the end of the book. Of course, the true value is NOT in the piece of paper. It's in the discussion and implementation of what is on the checklist.

On the topic of customer service, I would like to mention two others that I think do an outstanding job, Jeff Wandel and Mitch

Silveira. Jeff Wandel is the owner of the Big O Tire shop on Fourth Street in Santa Rosa and he has taken excellent care of the tires and brakes on all my vehicles for many years. Mitch Silveira, with Silveira Buick GMC dealership in Healdsburg, has helped me buy a number of cars over the years. Mitch has a helpful, no nonsense, no pressure style which I appreciate.

Key Takeaways

- 70% of family wealth erodes in the hands of the next generation.

- What's more valuable, money or knowledge? Having money is one thing; knowing how to make and keep it is another. Setting a long term direction and having a vision matter!

- Family wealth fails to last because families fall prey to serious money blunders. Take action to avoid the six common mistakes outlined in this chapter.

- Get the *57 Point Financial Health Checklist*. See the Free Resources page at the end of the book.

Chapter 9

Creating Wealth and Abundance

For the most part, my clients report major success using the suggestions you've just read about to create a pathway to a happy and secure lifestyle. But, as you might imagine, many people struggle with their very attitude about money. So, it's important that we talk about attitude—past, present and future.

Don't worry about your past. As Tony Robbins would say, *"The past does not equal the future."* Begin today to improve whatever isn't as you want it to be.

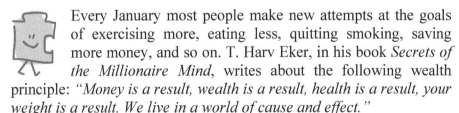

Every January most people make new attempts at the goals of exercising more, eating less, quitting smoking, saving more money, and so on. T. Harv Eker, in his book *Secrets of the Millionaire Mind*, writes about the following wealth principle: *"Money is a result, wealth is a result, health is a result, your weight is a result. We live in a world of cause and effect."*

Mr. Eker says that your financial blueprint consists of a combination of your thoughts, feelings, and actions, and it is the result of "programming" you received in the past, especially as a young child. To quote him on this:

97

"Isn't it true that certain cultures have one way of thinking and dealing with money, while other cultures have a different approach? Do you think a child comes out of the womb with his or her attitudes toward money, or do you believe the child is *taught* how to deal with money? That's right. Every child is taught how to think about and act in relation to money.

The same holds true for you, for me, for everyone. You were taught how to think and act when it comes to money. These teachings become your conditioning, which becomes automatic responses that run you for the rest of your life. Unless, of course, you intercede and revise your mind's money files.

Your programming leads to your thoughts; your thoughts lead to your feelings; your feelings lead to your actions; your actions lead to your results.

Therefore, just as is done with a personal computer, by changing your programming, you take the first essential step to changing your results."

So, if you're looking for different results, change your programming. It has to start there. Many good books and audio courses have been created for our improvement; it is a shame to let them go to waste! This reminds me of a little saying I read the other day, **"Learn More—Earn More."** I wrote that one on a Post-it. It is very similar to what Tom Hopkins, a world-renowned success coach, is famous for saying. He may have even said it to me when I met with him. What Tom says is, "If you want to earn more, it's a matter of learning more."

You Didn't Learn This in School

Our public school systems don't offer courses on creating prosperity or abundance, so we are basically left to guess at what the best ways are to create wealth. Unless you have deliberately sought out books, CDs, DVDs and seminars, or have been fortunate enough to have had mentors in your life who have shared with you this valuable information, you are on your own. You may have thought that just being lucky, working hard, or investing wisely would create wealth. You will agree that all these things are clearly helpful; however, I would like to share with you the knowledge I have acquired from being a student of prosperity. I have read many, many books on prosperity, listened to experts attentively, have gone to countless seminars, and have experimented with many different prosperity techniques. After all of this, my conclusion is that to become wealthy, other than by accident, birth, or marriage, requires the thinking about and doing of things others will not do.

You must have an open mind to consider new concepts. (These concepts are not really new, it is just that you were not taught them in any other influential environments.) You have to start by letting go of old beliefs that no longer serve you. The more open-minded you are, the more opportunities, thoughts, feelings, and perceptions can come to you on how to create real long term wealth.

Creating wealth and abundance has a lot to do with internal decisions and knowledge, and little to do with the state of the national economy. You must rise above the popular belief that you cannot avoid being affected by the economy! Abundance is a mindset, not an external condition that controls your destiny. There are no limits to what you can create, because you really do have unlimited resources in the power of your mind. I'm talking about determination here.

I recently spoke to Dan Ruettiger, the guy that the movie "Rudy" was made about, and I told him how inspired I was by his story. If you haven't seen this movie, I encourage you to watch it. It's a moving story about a kid who dreamed of playing football for Notre Dame. He didn't have the grades or the skill to make it…all he had was the determination. Isn't it cool how determination can trump everything that stands in our way?

Let's begin by defining wealth, at least by my own, more holistic view. Wealth is not just money, because creating money alone will not always bring you happiness. Wealth is being at peace with yourself and feeling fulfilled in what you do. It is enjoying and appreciating your life, your family, your friends and your business. Being rich is more than money or power. Being aware of this enables you to create more self-confidence, self-trust, and self-esteem. These new empowering traits will help you generate and create wealth and financial security.

Ralph Waldo Emerson described prosperity as the law of compensation whereby like attracts like, and what you radiate out in your thoughts, feelings, mental pictures, and words, you also attract in to your life. The truth is that we are where we are in our lives at this moment because of our past programming and the actions we do or don't take toward our ultimate goals.

History has recorded that more millionaires were created during the Great Depression than at any other time because of the infamous "poor economy." The people who believed in themselves were willing to take calculated risks. These people made tremendous amounts of money because they believed in themselves, looked for opportunities, TOOK ACTION and had prosperity consciousness. They did not let fate control their future—they took charge of their own destiny with their thoughts and actions!

They did not sit around thinking about what to do, but actually used their life energy to do what was necessary to achieve their dreams. They were not victims; they leveraged what they had into big success.

Many successful people say they make more money during a time of recession than when the economy is booming because other people run scared and sell out for less. The mass population tends to buy into media reports and financial experts' predictions of how bad the economy is or will be. When you buy into mass beliefs of poverty, you unknowingly disregard the opportunities you could have seen for creating wealth or happiness.

We are all influenced by our old programming—our self-image is created between the ages of three and seven by our teachers, parents, peers, and society. Some of the limiting programming we received on a daily basis were statements like *"The rich only get richer"* and *"This is a tough world"* and *"Money is the root of all evil."* You may not even be conscious of hearing and saying things like *"Everything happens to me," "The other guy is always lucky and gets all the breaks,"* or *"I can't win for losing."*

Start to pay attention to the quality of information you put into your brain; it truly is your success mechanism. What do <u>you</u> want your future to look like? Be conscious of what and who you allow in your head.

Good Habits to Develop:

- Step away from the people in your life who only focus on the negative. No one needs doomsday predictors. Yes, we all need balance and we need to know the pros and cons of all situations before we take action, but who needs the people who ONLY see the negative? Find new people to associate with who can actually assist you by inspiring you instead of depressing you and shooting down your aspirations.

- Pay attention to your self-talk. Your self-talk programs you for either poverty or prosperity consciousness. When you find yourself talking or thinking negatively, ask yourself: Do I really want to create this for my future? What am I focusing on? Is this leading me to my ultimate success or my ultimate failure? We are self-fulfilling prophecies.

- Turn off TV and radio news. Substitute educational materials to improve your outlook on life. Replace reading negative news with uplifting materials that give you ideas, suggestions, solutions and strategies to improve your life!

- Give yourself a technology break from social media sites, internet surfing, emails and texting. Why are you stressing yourself out and letting so much unnecessary and useless information clog up your thought processes? Be selective; these are tools for you to use, not a way of life.

In other words, take back your life. <u>You</u> are the creator of <u>your</u> reality with your thoughts and actions. Upgrade the caliber of information going into your brain.

Dream. Believe. Do.

As a person who loves goal setting, let me give you some encouragement in the area of planning and accomplishing goals. Your accomplishment of goals will mostly depend on your approach—and on your response when things are not going exactly as you planned. (Which they won't from time to time.) For example, popular New Year's resolutions are to lose weight and make more money—and make no mistake, everybody with these resolutions does very sincerely _want_ them. But when March comes (or when a few months pass) and you still weigh the same, don't give up! Reassess your methods (not your goals) and try again!

The opportunities to accomplish these goals, and others, are not under lock and key and doled out only to a favored few. It's not an absence of desire or opportunity which causes your lack of achievement. It's not what you _want_. Nor, for most, is it where you live, or even what business you are in. It's what you do. What YOU do. What you DO.

So, if you're still a little fuzzy on the plan for this year, or the next five years, I encourage you to make this the year that you take control of your money—and your life. DO whatever it takes.

Gordon Gekko, I'm Not

You may think from reading my books, newspaper columns, magazine articles and newsletters that I'm a money-hungry, capitalist pig, akin to Gordon Gekko. (From the movie *Wall Street*, played by Michael Douglas.) But you'd be very wrong. And you're probably glad I'm saying that.

Gordon says, "*Greed is good,*" and he's building an empire to match his ego. He would agree with J. Paul Getty, who, when asked, "*How much is enough?*" answered, "*Just a little bit more.*"

I think it's pretty natural for a CPA who specializes in wealth management vocationally to talk at length about building and preserving wealth. But there is a difference between being a shrewd steward of your resources and being one who builds bigger barns merely for the sake of having bigger barns.

The difference is in your heart. I see it in people's attitudes, what they value, their pride and their generosity. Personally, I like to think that I put people first and live my life fully aware that there will be no U-Haul trailer behind my hearse.

However, I do think we should be smart in our financial dealings, and always look to grow and protect the assets we have, for the current and future needs of ourselves and our loved ones. There is honor in providing for the needs of the loved ones who depend on us. That's what I like to help clients do.

There is a story worth reading from The New York Times (July 1998) about Donald and Mildred Othmer, who amassed a fortune over their lifetimes. They did not worry about financial matters, because they lived within their means and saved the excess. They left hundreds of millions to charities through their estate. Their legacy lives on through the lives they've helped. (Google this for the rest of their story.)

Others find opportunity during economic downturns. The Kennedy, Rothschild and Rockefeller families and Howard Hughes all made huge fortunes during the Great Depression—and they were just the famous ones! Many other lesser known folks also accumulated big money in those troubled times, while others came out of the Great Depression dirt poor. Our current economy may be a similar time in history and provide a similar wealth-building opportunity for those who are aware. Hopefully, your goal will not just be to build yourself a bigger barn, but instead to leave a lasting legacy as a generous humanitarian.

Eureka!

Getting rich quick can be liberating, but it can also be frustrating. Sudden wealth can help you resolve anxieties about funding your retirement or your children's college educations. Newfound financial freedom can lead to time freedom— greater opportunity to live and work on your terms. On the other hand, you'll pay more taxes, attract more attention and maybe even contend with jealousy or envy from certain friends and relatives. You may have to deal with grief or stress, as a lump sum may be linked to a death, a divorce or a pension payout decision.

Windfalls don't always lead to happy endings. Take the example of Bud Post, who won more than $16 million in the Pennsylvania lottery in 1988. Eighteen years later, he passed away owing more than $1 million after business failures and bad investments. Along the way, his girlfriend successfully sued him for some of the money and his brother hired a hit man to try and take him out, hoping to inherit some of those assets. That weird and tragic example aside, windfalls don't necessarily breed "old money" either. Without long-range vision, one generation's wealth may not transfer to the next. As mentioned earlier, according to the *Wall Street Journal*, on average 70% of the wealth built by one generation is lost by the next. Two generations later, an average of 90% of it disappears.

So what are some wise steps to take when you receive a windfall? What might you do to keep that money in your life and in your family for years to come?

 Keep quiet, if you can. If you aren't in the spotlight, don't step into it. Who really needs to know about your newfound wealth besides you and your immediate family? The IRS, the financial professionals whom you consult or hire, and your attorney. The list needn't be much longer, and you may want to limit it to that.

 What if you can't keep it quiet? Winning a lottery prize, selling your company, signing a multiyear deal—when your wealth is publicized, expect friends and strangers to come knocking at your door. Be fair, firm and friendly—and avoid handling the requests yourself. (That first, generous handout may risk opening the floodgate to subsequent handout requests.) Let your financial team review loan requests, business proposals, and pipe dreams.

 Yes, your *team*. If big money comes your way, you need skilled professionals in your corner—a CPA, an attorney and a wealth manager. Ideally your CPA is a tax advisor, your lawyer is an estate planning attorney, and your wealth manager pays attention to tax efficiency and helps you keep <u>and</u> grow your new wealth.

 Think this through in stages. When a big lump sum enhances your financial standing, you need to think about the present, the near future, and the decades ahead. Many people celebrate their good fortune when they receive sudden wealth and live in the moment, only to wonder years later where that moment (and their money) went.

In the present, an infusion of wealth may give you some tax dilemmas; it may also require you to reconsider existing beneficiary designations on your IRAs, retirement plans, investment accounts and insurance policies. Your will, your trust, your existing estate plan— they may need to be revisited. Resist the temptation to try and grow the newly acquired wealth quickly through aggressive investing.

Now, how about the next few years? What does financial independence (or greater financial freedom) mean for you? How do you want to spend your time? Should you continue in your present career? Should you stick with your business or sell or transfer ownership? What kinds of near-term possibilities could this open up for you? What are the concrete financial steps that could help you defer or reduce taxes in the next few years? How can risk be sensibly managed as some or all of the assets are invested? I encourage you to seek professional advice.

Looking further ahead, tax efficiency can potentially make an enormous difference for that lump sum. You may end up with considerably more money (or considerably less) decades from now due to asset location and other tax factors.

Think about doing nothing for a while. Nothing financially momentous, that is. There's nothing wrong with that. Sudden, impulsive moves with sudden wealth can backfire.

Welcome the positive financial changes, but don't change yourself. Remaining true to your morals, ethics and beliefs will help you stay grounded. Turning to professionals who know how to capably guide that wealth is just as vital.

Key Takeaways

- As Tony Robbins would say, *"The past does not equal the future."* Begin today to improve whatever isn't as you want it to be.

- T. Harv Eker says, *"Money is a result, wealth is a result, health is a result, your weight is a result. We live in a world of cause and effect."* If you're looking for different results—change your programming.

- Creating wealth and abundance has more to do with internal decisions and knowledge, and less to do with the state of the national economy.

- Wealth is being at peace with yourself and feeling fulfilled in what you do. It is enjoying and appreciating your life, your family, and your business. Being rich is more than money or power.

- Pay attention to the quality of information you put into your brain; it truly is your success mechanism.

- Windfalls don't always lead to happy endings. Proceed cautiously, with professional advice.

SECTION II

BONUS CHAPTERS FROM GUEST EXPERTS

Introduction by
Montgomery Taylor

Over the years, I've built successful CPA and Wealth Management firms and written and taught a fair amount on financial topics. The knowledge base for these endeavors is vast and complex and changes each time Congress meets. To keep up, I read a lot, attend educational events, get some coaching and seek the guidance of certain experts. I have various relationships with the experts presented here. Some are clients of mine. Some provide advice or services to me or my clients. They were each hand-picked because they bring a different viewpoint and a different opportunity, as well as authority, expertise, and experience to the total discussion of happiness and security in Sonoma County.

Perhaps this writing experience will encourage them to write more. Personally, I was encouraged to keep writing by Jack Canfield, who is responsible for the fabulously successful *Chicken Soup for the Soul* book series, along with co-author Mark Victor Hansen. I was fortunate to meet Mr. Canfield last year and discuss my book writing with him. I'm sharing that inspiration with my guest experts here in this joint effort.

Including them here does not transfer any liability or responsibility to me or to this book's publisher for any decisions you make, actions you take, or relationships you enter into as a result of reading this book, because each individual's circumstances are different. **<u>You</u> are 100% responsible for your own financial, business and life decisions.** If unwilling to accept such responsibility, you should read no further. And, should you be in doubt about any investment-related decision or similar matter, the counsel and services of appropriate professionals, such as your own CPA or attorney, should be sought.

Readers, you are each at a different place in terms of age, experience, income, wealth, available time, risk tolerance, initiative, interest in active or passive investments, etc., and you each must think independently and arrive at your own way, the right way for your circumstances.

In this section, you will discover experts, opportunities, and opinions—including a few opinions not in perfect harmony with everything I've said in the previous section of this book. All of it is for the purpose of stimulating you to think—not to tell you **what** to think!

These authors, myself included, want to serve you as models, mentors or coaches. Any way that you will allow, we're here to lift you up.

Chapter 10

Mortgaging Your Way to Financial Security

Rich Abazia

By a fortunate stroke of luck I found myself in Sonoma County in 1975. Arriving with $200 and a guitar, only knowing one person, a fellow musician, and having my sights set on moving to another state made no difference. I knew instantly I had found paradise. During my years in Sonoma County, I have met many people and have had the great fortune to call several of them mentors. After working in a few different professions, by chance I found myself in the mortgage industry in 1986.

In my profession I hear all kinds of stories, meet the most interesting people and gain insight into how people move their lives along. I am also able to see their mistakes and their successes. My clients, John and Mary, had plenty of both.

John and Mary wanted to purchase their first home. They were already middle-aged when I met them. John was a retired flooring tradesman and Mary had worked in a medical office. They had saved a modest amount of money, were tired of paying rent and wanted to finally have a place of their own. We met at my office to "pre-approve" them for a mortgage so they would have an idea of what they could qualify for and which price range to look in.

When I interview folks, there are four basic items I always cover. I call them the "Four legs of a loan." They are: income, credit, down payment and property. I use a chair as a metaphor. A chair has four legs, but if one of those legs is weak your chair starts getting wobbly. The same is true for a home loan.

Being a flooring tradesman is tough on the body and John's knees were shot. He left that trade and found a new job, in a new profession. His income, although modest, was stable. Mary's job was solid. They were good, hardworking people and their combined income was enough to handle the mortgage payment. They had also saved a modest amount of money, enough to make a 10% down payment, but found they would have very few reserves left after making the down payment. Reserves are so important—everybody should plan for that "rainy day" and put money aside for retirement. Great! Two legs of the loan covered. The property would come later, so we moved on to check their credit.

Readers, life happens. No matter how much control you think you have, life can throw you a curve, and in John and Mary's case it was about health issues. They had maxed out their credit cards, medical bills had piled up, and they were getting calls from collection agencies. Their credit was not in the best shape. Although their medical insurance plan would eventually cover most of the expenses, many of the doctors had been quick to send bills to the collection agencies. This often happens when insurance companies are slow to pay the doctors. Additionally, they had co-signed loans with their adult children which had resulted in a mess on their credit report. Their chair was wobbling! We had our work cut out for us.

One of the most important aspects of obtaining a loan is your credit score. This is also known as your "FICO" score—named after Fair Isaac Company, who pioneered the mathematical algorithm.

Basically the score is a forward-looking indicator of the likelihood of the borrower defaulting on a loan in the next two years. The scores range from 350 at the low end to 850 at the high end. Like bowling, higher is better.

There are five categories that comprise your credit score, each having a percentage attached to it:

1. Payment history, 35%. Do you pay on time? A recent late payment hurts more than a bankruptcy 5 years ago.

2. Credit utilization, 30%. How do you use your credit? Are you at your credit limit on a few credit cards? It may be better to have smaller balances on more cards than to max out a few cards.

3. Length of credit history, 15%. How long have you had an account? The longer you have a credit account in good standing, the better your score.

4. New credit, 10%. Do you credit "surf" from one card to another? It looks desperate if you do. Don't max out new credit cards.

5. Types of credit used, 10%. Have you had to resort to finance companies for auto loans and other consumer loans? These kinds of credit usually involve higher interest rates and do not improve your credit score.

Back to John and Mary. Their credit scores were low because they had past due accounts, collections, and a mess due to co-signed delinquent credit. I told them, quite frankly, that if they did not work on getting their credit profile under control they would be stuck in a high interest rate credit quagmire for the rest of their lives. This is the reality we live in: the higher the risk, the higher the interest rate, and the higher the monthly payments. They looked at each other for a long time. *This was their chance to grab hold of their future and take control.* We mapped out a two year strategy. They would buy a home now, with a high interest loan, and then clean up their credit and use any future equity to help pay off their debt and put some money away for retirement.

One of the first items on the list was to quit co-signing loans for their adult children. Their adult children did not pay their bills on time, which reflected poorly on John and Mary's credit. They asked their children to refinance all of their co-signed auto loans into their own names and had them pay off and close all of the other co-signed credit cards. This took some time but the "kids" made it happen. John and Mary actually did a great service to their adult children by forcing them to take a look at their own credit behavior and take control of their own spending.

John and Mary made arrangements with the creditors to have their payments reduced to a level they could afford. They also contacted their medical insurance company and various collection agencies regarding the unpaid doctors' bills. They put pressure on the insurance company to pay the doctors in a timely manner and also contacted the doctors and asked them to please not send the bills to collections. Their credit card balances were quite large and they could only afford the minimum payments. At credit card interest rates of 25% or more, it would have taken a lifetime to pay off the debt. Additionally they had no reserves set aside and we needed to address that. Sometimes there is too much month left at the end of the money!

During the next year or so I checked periodically on John and Mary and I found that they were setting aside a modest amount of money every month for retirement. Additionally they were making headway on paying off their debt, although there was still a long way to go. On the upside, they just loved their home, had fantastic neighbors and truly enjoyed having family and friends over for cook outs and dinner parties. Life was good. After some time I asked an appraiser friend of mine to give me an opinion as to what John and Mary's home was worth. I was happily surprised to hear their home had increased in value quite a bit. With the increased equity in the property it was time to implement the final part of the plan.

I asked John and Mary to visit with me at my office. It was nice to catch up with them and to see how their lives had changed for the better. I checked their credit score and was happily surprised to see that it had gone from 580 to 720. Wow! All of the credit nasties were gone and there were no more delinquent co-signed loans. The credit agencies were satisfied and all creditors were reporting paid as agreed.

It had taken them two years, but their chair was steady again and they had managed to do it on their own!

It was finally time to refinance their home. Why do people refinance their homes? They do it for a number of reasons: to lower monthly payments, to purchase income producing assets, to fund retirement and/or college accounts, to pay off consumer debt and to make home improvements. John and Mary did all of that. They took some cash out of their equity to pay off and close their credit accounts, fund a retirement account, invest in some solid mutual funds and make some home improvements. And their monthly payment was still lower than it had been with the high interest loan!

I cautioned them about going back to their old spending ways (no globe-trotting yet!) with the new found money coming into their pocket every month. "No way," they said, "It took us two hard years to dig out from that mess and we're not going back."

Now many years later I still see John around town. I often think of them as an example of how my clients can turn their lives around and vastly improve their financial security and personal happiness. They have:

- managed their credit,
- bought a home,
- funded a retirement account,
- purchased some mutual funds,
- and are living happily ever after!

You're not going to get this kind of professional service from an online mortgage lender, that's for sure! But you will from me. Come in and chat—I'll ask you some questions and you'll have some for me. Together we will see if a new or better mortgage will be your path to improved financial security.

Three Big Questions

When listening to my clients I often hear questions in the same three areas. They have frequently tried to find answers to these questions themselves, but ended up even more confused. There is so much information available these days—some good, some misguided, and some truly awful! Let me throw some light on these issues.

What's the advantage of a local vs. an online mortgage company?

Surfing the Internet for a new mortgage sounds like a great idea. You can do it at 2:00 a.m. when you can't sleep, on a Saturday morning while your spouse is in bed, or at work when your boss is not looking. You can wear your jammies, have bed hair, and not even bother to shave, brush your teeth or do your makeup. Why go to the bother of making an appointment, taking time off from work, dealing with day care, gathering up your spouse and driving across town to sit in someone's office?

You probably want value for your hard earned money. So do I. The reality with online mortgage companies is that they really don't offer tremendous savings. Your local mortgage consultant and the big online players all go to the same pool of money for your mortgage. But your local mortgage consultant can also help direct you to the right product for you, as there is more to a loan than the interest rate. The online companies are merely order takers. They process your loan in a centralized location and don't offer much hand holding.

I also think it is important to support the local economy and put local people to work. Your finances and personal information are much too important to trust out in the cyberspace. You will be much happier in the long run if you use a local broker. (And I don't mind if you wear your jammies to my office!)

Should I pay off my mortgage early or have a mortgage in retirement?

This is something I am asked constantly. I believe there are many advantages in keeping a mortgage. Most important is the mortgage interest deduction on your income taxes. Currently Uncle Sam provides a tax write-off for a portion of the interest you pay. When you factor in the low interest rates we have seen over the past few years and the tax deduction, your effective interest rate is pretty low. Heck, it's almost free. For example, if you have a 4.5% interest rate and receive 33% of that as a tax deduction, you are effectively paying 3% for your loan! It is much more important to pay off consumer interest (credit cards, etc.) which can have interest rates of 25% or more, offer no tax benefits and make the banks more profitable. Make your mortgage work for you. We all like to save money on taxes! Money saved now can add up to improved financial security later.

What is leverage and what can it do for me?

Leverage is using your mortgage as a tool to purchase other income producing assets. This can include funding a retirement account, paying for a college education or buying a second home or rental property. We have historically record-low interest rates right now. If you can take this cheap money and get a higher return elsewhere, this makes good financial sense.

And don't forget to invest in yourself—use your mortgage to take that African safari, a tour of Tuscany or the Caribbean cruise you've been thinking of. We all need to live a little! It is possible to take equity out of your home for this purpose, but remember that your home equity can be an important source of financial security and don't use it all up to go globe-trotting. You should look at your home as a happy place to live first, and then as security for you and your family. But remember that it is not an open-ended piggy bank to fund an out-of-control lifestyle.

I have the best job in the world. I help people. I help them achieve their dreams through proper mortgage planning. My clients are the most interesting people: Super Lotto winners, business owners, first time home buyers, wonderful families, and good old hard working folks like John and Mary. I have been fortunate to work in this field for such a long time and am happy to say that many of my clients who were with me from the beginning are still clients of mine today. Now I get to work with my clients' children and even grandchildren.

Each client brings such a different perspective and history, and they have taught me a few things over the years. I've learned that hard and smart work pays off. I have seen the power of taking control of your life. John and Mary showed me the value of having the strength to tackle your own problems and not look for handouts, to make something of your life and provide for the lives of your children. It's part of the American way and it's also a road map for living happily and securely in Sonoma County...Oh, and that guitar? I still have it and play it when I am not making home loans.

About Rich

Rich Abazia is the Broker/Owner of Cypress Financial Mortgage. Rich currently holds a California Real Estate Broker's license. Previously he has held three securities licenses and a life insurance license as well as a contractor's license. Rich grew up in northern New Jersey where he attended William Patterson University as a political science major. When not making home loans, Rich can be found playing music, fishing and travelling. He has visited over 30 countries, is fluent in Swedish and is an accomplished guitarist and multi-instrumentalist. He has recorded music in the USA and in Europe, has studied guitar with Danny Kalb of the Blues Project, Eddie Simon (Paul Simons' brother), as well as many blues artists. He currently plays in a classic rock and roll band when not making home loans.

Rich has been in the mortgage industry for 28 years. In 1995 he opened Cypress Financial Mortgage. In the years 2002 and 2003 Rich was honored as "one of the year's top 10 mortgage brokers in the country" by the Federal Home Loan Mortgage Corporation (Freddie Mac). This honor was the result of his use of technology in obtaining a high degree of loan approvals for his clients. In 2014 Rich earned the "Lending Integrity Seal of Approval" awarded by the National Association of Mortgage Brokers. The seal recognizes individual brokers who meet the industry's highest standards for knowledge, professionalism, ethics and integrity. Rich specializes in residential financing as well as commercial and construction loans. A Sonoma County resident since 1974, Rich and his family make their home in Santa Rosa, California.

Chapter 11

Aging in Sonoma County: Living the Healthy, Happy Life at Home

Lucy Andrews, RN, MS

On the outside, the suburban home, although shabby with age, was fairly tidy. But inside, the stench of rotting meat and garbage hit me with full force. It wasn't completely unexpected after the call from Carol: "I am at the end of my rope, and I don't know what to do. I've been trying to care for my elderly mother myself but I just can't do it. Before I give up I thought I would call you. Can you help me?"

Carol told me that her mother, Grace, had been diagnosed with dementia and as the disease progressed had begun hoarding things. It had gotten out of control and mother and daughter were at a stalemate. When I arrived at the house Carol quickly apologized for the awful smell and pointed towards the kitchen. "It's in there. She puts all the meat in the fridge, not the freezer. She ate something really bad a few days ago and was sick. And she won't throw anything away."

While situations like this don't occur every day, they happen all too often. Carol and I created a plan for Grace, and step by step, we implemented it. We replaced the bad food with good, we substantially cleared the cluttered rooms, and with trust and time Grace has come to welcome our caregivers.

No one wants to think of getting old and losing the ability to be independent. We all want to walk without assistance, remember our own family members, run our own affairs, and live where we choose. If you think "Oh no, it's all doom and gloom!" think again! There are a few simple things you can do today to ensure that you and your loved ones are prepared for the future. This chapter will give you great tips on staying healthy, happy and at home in Sonoma County.

Having some control over the aging process and making your wishes known are two of the healthiest and more proactive things you can do today to make tomorrow enjoyable! Sometimes it's a hard conversation even with yourself, but in the end, it's worth it. With a bit of soul searching, planning, and documenting, you can lift up the burden of the future and be happier as you age.

First, a little bit about how I look at aging, some tips I have learned over the years, and how I got into the field of helping people to live happy and healthy lives at home (and to die there when the time comes.)

For the past 24 years I have worked as a home care and hospice nurse. I love the independence that working with patients in their homes brings me. I find great reward and satisfaction in making a real difference in people's lives over the long term—not just for that short stay in the hospital. I also know home is where people want to be even during an illness. Long ago I realized something was missing in our health system. People were not staying at home as they aged—they often ended up in institutional care (code for nursing homes), a place where no one wants to live.

What they really needed was help at home: a watchful eye, somebody checking on them and making sure that all was well. Often they just needed help with the little things like preparing meals or getting to the grocery store or just having a companion.

This was the missing link—the thing that really helped to make a difference in keeping loved ones or family members at home, where they wanted to be. I realized my passion was helping people (myself included) at home! I started At Your Service Home Care on sweat equity, a bit of savings and my passion for helping people to stay at home, living long productive lives. That was in 2003 and we have now helped over a thousand families in Sonoma County to stay healthy and happy at home. It has been a true gift and has led to great satisfaction for me personally. I have been allowed to be a part of families, joining in the joys and sorrows that surround caring for loved ones. Each family's circumstance is different and each person's wish is unique. The important thing is to plan in advance and have time to enjoy each other.

Learning from my own experiences, and paying attention to the needs of the families we cared for, I found recurrent issues surfacing. I formulated tips that you can apply to your own life, so that you can have the future you <u>want</u>, not the one that happens to you because you didn't have a plan.

You can't tell someone else your wishes for your own positive aging if you are not clear on what you want. Here are a few basic questions to ask yourself. Take some time and think about your answers. You may find they change as you sift through your own emotional landscape and think about your own future.

- What do I want to happen to me if I am ill and can't speak for myself?

- Who should make health care and other decisions if I cannot make them?

- Where do I want to age—at my present home or somewhere else?

- Who should my caregiver be? A family member, my spouse or a paid professional?

The answers to the first two questions are ones which should be put into legal documents such as an Advance Health Care Directive.

Consult your family attorney or complete the state approved forms to make your wishes known. Give a copy to your physician, and perhaps to a family member. Ask your physician or local hospital for these forms, or get them at:

www.oag.ca.gov/consumers/general/adv_hc_dir

Your attorney is also the person to talk with about estate planning and naming your Executor. It is never a good idea to have only one set of eyes on your affairs. Never use a paid caregiver as your executor.

The third question, "Where do I want to live as I age?" is a much bigger question. Your answers will be different from mine, or your spouse's or even your children's. This is why it is important to ask and answer these questions for yourself, before the crisis comes and before someone has to guess what your wishes are. Remember that even if you put something into a legal document it is changeable, as your wishes are not irrevocable. You are different now from whom you were as a young adult and you may feel differently in another ten or twenty years. You can change your mind and your answers; at least you will be miles ahead by already having asked the questions!

So what does it really take to live at home well into your nineties and beyond? Well, it takes a village and it starts with planning. Let's start with your physical location. There are many factors to consider in determining if your current home is the right place to stay. Should you stay there or downsize and move to a smaller home or into community living? Should you move closer to a family member? There are many options. If you think you may not be physically able to stay at home, now is the time to think about the future.

We cared for Al, a lovely gentleman who had lived in his home for 70 years. It was a beautiful house, remote and nestled in the trees, filled with art and family treasures. But—there were multiple levels, loads of steps and very narrow hallways. It was great if you loved Frank Lloyd Wright's style, but it was a bear if you had to use a walker down the hallway to the bathroom. Al started falling and had many close calls. Finally, his family insisted that he move to a facility where the wide hallways had rails and he did not have to navigate stairs. He didn't want to go, to leave his home of so many years, but things were heading toward a crisis and his family felt he was not safe. He was heartbroken but reluctantly moved from his beloved home. With just a little more proactive planning and a bit more communication Al might have stayed in his home.

Answering these questions before a crisis could have helped Al, and could help you too.

- How many steps or levels does the house have?

- Can modifications be made? Can a ramp be installed?

- Can a dining room or office be converted into a downstairs bedroom to avoid using the stairs?

- Are the bathrooms big enough to fit a wheelchair or walker? Can hand rails, a raised toilet, and a shower seat be installed?

- Is there a place close by the bedroom where a caregiver might sleep?

- What if public transportation is needed in the future? Is the neighborhood served by a public bus or para-transport route?

Your answers will guide you in determining the suitability of your home and help you determine your future. Making small or even large modifications may be the answer. Grab bars, additional lighting and non-slip treads for steps are just a few of the things you can do without much effort or cost.

If you find your home may not be suitable in the future, now is the time to start planning the alternatives. Remodeling or downsizing to a different house (or home alternative) are discussions to have as a whole family. This is where the village comes in. Use the counsel of family and trusted advisors to look at all the alternatives available. I encourage you to think outside of the box and keep the conversation going!

Once you have the physical location issues handled, the next complex question to address is the one of care. If your physical health changes, you may need a few hours a day or a few days a week of care. One of the biggest challenges is being able to afford it. What if you need around-the-clock care at home? Will it be possible? Let's talk finances. Care at home can be a very expensive proposition. With a bit of planning (and that village), you can stay where you are, aging in place at home, where we all want to be.

As I work with the adult children of our clients, they are struck by the decisions they have to make for someone else. What I hear is "I am looking at my own future differently now. I want to make sure I have my finances in order when I am my parents' age." Here are a few things that you can do now to make sure you can afford to have your wishes and needs met. I recommend consulting a professional for help answering these questions. Planning now and being ready for that "rainy day" is critical for remaining healthy, happy and secure in Sonoma County.

1. Look at your retirement funds and expected future earnings—will your budget include money for care? What are your current and future options on retirement? How can you increase your nest egg? How long will you need, want, and be able to work?

2. Do you have long term care insurance? If you have a policy, review it. Will it meet your needs? If you don't have one, consider one as an option for funding future care.

3. What is the cost of care? Don't underestimate this cost, as twenty-four hour home care currently can run almost $10,000 per month. Will a family member be available to care for you? You might assume some portion of future care may be paid for by health insurance or Medicare, but beware: they do not pay for this type of service. This out-of-pocket expense can greatly impact your future financial security!

So now you have a future plan that you can work on, but what if you need to care for a loved one right now? What if that "rainy day" is today? (And yes, it is going to rain one day!) There are things you can do to make caring for a loved one a meaningful, positive, and healthy event. If you are the primary care provider it is so important to make sure that you remain healthy and happy. This means taking care of your needs as well as looking after someone else's needs.

Often families fall apart when the primary care provider becomes exhausted and overwhelmed with the demands of caring for a loved one. Make sure you are getting all your medical needs met— keep up on your routine health care, take your medications and get scheduled tests done. After all, if you are not healthy you can't care for someone else. Take time for yourself. Try to use all the time-saving tools at your disposal, such as home delivery of groceries, prescriptions refilled by mail, and a housekeeper at least once a month. <u>Now</u> you are a caregiver, but you are <u>still</u> a spouse or partner, a child, or a friend. Take time to be what you were to each other before the current crisis.

Get help from the community. There are many support groups and resources available in this great spot where we live. Sonoma County offers resources in the form of support groups like those listed on **www.alz.org**. At the website for Senior Advocacy Services, **www.senioradvocacyservices.org**, you can find information on medical services, assisted living, transportation and many other free resources.

If you use family members as care providers, set up realistic expectations before they start and keep the communication going. If there are differing opinions on care, sometimes the sanest option is to hire a home care agency to assume responsibility for providing and supervising caregivers. This option also avoids burnout and resentments that can arise from being a caregiver <u>and</u> a family member.

Finally, take time to get support. Caring for a loved one is not to be done as a solo sport! This is the most important tip I can give you. Make sure you have a support system in place. Friends, family or professionals all can help ease your responsibilities. We are very lucky we live in an area where we have so many community resources and services. Take advantage of them.

At Your Service Home Care is here to help—let us be part of your village. If you are wondering what your next step is, call us. We offer a free in-home safety evaluation, and can answer your questions about preparing for your future and caring for your loved one. We will help you sort out your options so you can take a breath and re-focus on what's important. In my own family, having help allowed me to spend time with my elderly mother <u>and</u> keep all the balls in the air going.

Remember that we all want a secure happy future, aging well at home. Using these tips will help you achieve your goals. They will serve you well now and in the future. If you are caring for a loved one as you read this, make sure you take care of yourself, stay healthy and engage the support systems around you. You will be happier and healthier in the long run!

About Lucy

Lucy Andrews is the founder and CEO of At Your Service Home Care, a concierge home care agency that provides essential services for seniors to age in place. With 33 years experience as a nurse and patient advocate, she offers a high level of care, allowing people to be in their own homes with an emphasis on independence, safety, and quality of life.

Lucy has a degree in Nursing from Lewis University and an M.S. in Health Service Administration from St. Mary's University, and will graduate with her Doctorate in Nursing Practice in March 2017. She has served on the boards for both State and National Home Care Associations; is currently the Vice Chair of the Board of Directors, National Association for Home Care and Hospice; and on the Board of Directors, California State Association for Health Care At Home. Lucy goes to Washington, DC, several times a year to advocate for senior services and home care issues. She also served on our local Senior Advocacy Services Board and on the board for CHANGE, a local horse rescue group.

Living in East Santa Rosa with her husband and family, Lucy is a proud mother and grandmother. They share their home with many rescued animals which hold special spots in her heart.

Chapter 12

How Can I Be Happy and Secure If My Spouse Wants a Divorce?

Jeanne Browne, Esq.

You were blind-sided, you had no clue, and you don't understand how this could have happened to you. Your wife just told you she hasn't loved you for years and she wants a divorce. She wanted counseling years ago, but you didn't want some shrink telling you how to run your life. How could she do this to you? She knows you're a good provider, working overtime to pay the bills, repair the house, and hey, you even took the whole family to Disney World last year. What's not to love? Will some red roses change her mind? Unfortunately, she already moved out with the kids.

Maybe instead you are that devoted wife who noticed your husband's cell phone bill had a repeated unfamiliar number logged while he was working late. You swallow hard as you call the number, hoping you are overreacting. A woman answers. Your husband's later explanation confirms your worst fear: "She was my high school sweetheart. I never stopped loving her." He found her on Facebook, or was it through his Match.com profile? Your heart thuds, and you go numb inside, unable to think straight for months.

While these stories are changed to protect the innocent (or the guilty), they reveal life-changing events that threaten our security and happiness. Your situation might involve less trauma because your children are grown and you've made a mutual decision to separate. But you may still be asking "Where do I go from here?"

As a family law attorney in Santa Rosa for over 25 years, my job is to help separating or divorcing couples navigate through similar painful situations. My goal is to make a positive difference for clients and their children who are surrounded by swirling emotional tides beneath their ocean of legal issues. The undertow of the breakup snatches away their trust, and waves of doubt crash over their rock of security. They need a safe harbor to repair their human vessel and make it seaworthy again.

I experienced a "simple" divorce in my early twenties, but thankfully I have not had to endure what many of my clients experience. I have been remarried now for 32 years to my wonderful husband Bill and we have two grown daughters. My family moved to Petaluma when I was 10 years old and I have lived in Sonoma County ever since. I attended Sonoma State University's paralegal program before obtaining my law degree from Empire Law School. These accomplishments could not have happened without encouragement from my husband and family, and my faith in God's constant guidance.

Questions that divorcing clients often ask me are:

- Will a judge make all the decisions or can my spouse and I agree on our own?

- How can we get through this separation or divorce without financial and emotional ruin?

- How can we best protect our children in this difficult time?

To help answer these questions, allow me to share five important principles and an easy way to remember them—it's as easy as referencing the five fingers on your hand. Let's start with your thumb.

1. Encouragement: Thumb

First, give yourself a "thumbs up" as a reminder that you can get through this and not be overwhelmed. If you were my client I would encourage you to surround yourself with positive emotional support. Realistically, I usually compare the divorce process with a roller coaster—the "Big D Dipper"—with unexpected velocity, extreme highs and lows, abrupt direction changes, and plenty of screaming!

You will need reassurance from friends and family to avoid depression or self-medicating behaviors. "Encourage one another and build each other up." This biblical reference reminds me to do this for others. If you don't have an "encourager" in your life, join a divorce support group. You may also need a trained therapist with divorce expertise. Think of him or her as your emotional "safety harness" to keep you from revenge or subversive tactics (like slashing tires or sending that nasty text you will later regret!) You need to learn how to "keep your hands and arms inside" until this shaky ride comes to a complete stop.

2. Direction: Pointer Finger

How do you feel when I point my finger "at" you? (No, not the middle finger, I already know that answer!) If I stick my index finger in your face, do you feel defensive? Am I instigating a fight? Better to use this finger to point "outward" to offer "direction" instead.

If I was new to Sonoma County and I asked you, a long-time resident, for the quickest route to Johnny Garlic's restaurant and the best time to catch my favorite cooking celebrity there, wouldn't you point the way, and mention your favorite entrée? I hope so! If you have experience in local fine dining or know the best winery tours, I would want you to share that information.

If you came to my office for family law advice, I would point out the different roads available. My job is to educate you about each process and help you decide which method is best for you.

The three main roads are litigation, mediation, and collaborative practice. Litigation is familiar to anyone who watches TV (thanks to shows like Boston Legal or The Good Wife). The judge reviews the evidence and decides. In divorce, no matter how fair a judge is, there are no "winners" and there is almost always collateral damage: for example, time away from work, lost income, attorney fees and other costs, and missed opportunities with your children. Sometimes it is appropriate to choose litigation if you need a temporary restraining order immediately, or if you need to fight a vicious litigation attorney helping your ex to get his or her "pound of flesh."

Other available roads that bypass the court house are mediation and collaborative practice. These focus on helping parties reach mutually acceptable and private solutions with neutral professional guidance, without giving up decision-making power to a stranger. Yes, you can make your own agreements with your spouse.

In mediation, one neutral attorney guides the parties through their own decision-making process, and does not "legally represent" either spouse. Creative ideas are exchanged in a series of meetings at an attorney/mediator's office over the period of a few weeks or months. Financial information is jointly gathered; no one makes court appearances. Mediation offers a good solution for parties who can sit in the same room, respectfully stating their needs and goals for resolution.

For example, as a mediator, I have encountered couples unable to agree about who should keep the diamond wedding ring. If the wife wants it, the husband wants her to pay him half of the value or sell it. To the wife, the sentimental value exceeds its actual value. One couple ended up agreeing to the wife keeping the ring in exchange for the husband keeping his vehicle without financial offset; another couple decided to give it to their grown daughter. Their individual needs were met in both situations. Using legal standards, a judge would not have made these same rulings.

While mediators cannot give legal "advice" (recommend a decision for either person), a discussion about statutes and case law can occur and be helpful. Once agreement is reached, the mediator will draft a Marital Settlement Agreement and court documents listing the parties as "self represented." Mediators are duty-bound to instruct each spouse to consult with independent counsel before they sign this important contract, just to confirm they understand the agreement. Statistics reveal that mediation is often less expensive than litigation. It is also more durable because the parties are more likely to follow a settlement they created on their own; there is no reason to appeal because the judge didn't decide for them.

Getting clear direction is especially important for overlapping issues of tax implications, estate planning, bankruptcy, real estate, or investment strategies. There are excellent Sonoma County professional resources listed in this book, so use them!

3. Responsibility: Middle Finger

As we already addressed, it's best not to point with this finger! Note instead that it is the tallest finger on your hand; let's have it represent a leader "standing tall" for what is right and taking responsibility for making the right choice.

Now let's address that question of how best to protect your children during this difficult time of transition. If your daughter was running into the street and a truck was coming toward her, wouldn't you take responsibility to run and grab her? Of course you would! It is equally important for you to protect your daughters and sons from emotional harm. Like it or not, this includes refraining from calling your ex names, arguing, yelling, or slinging snide remarks or angry looks at each other during custody exchanges. Even if you think your children can't hear or see you, they know the contempt you have for their other parent. Lead with integrity and self-discipline, even if your soon-to-be ex does not.

Your lifelong assignment is to encourage your children's relationship with their mom or dad. They are 50% of you and 50% of the other parent, so please realize that "talking smack" about your ex is referring also to them. Remind your children (even grown children) that you both love them and that the divorce is not, and never was, their fault. You want to be invited when they get married, right? Show you can behave. Remove any fear that one of you may ruin a special day by making a scene.

Take responsibility by looking through the lens the court uses—the "children's best interests." You may want them to go back and forth between houses every two days, but it is usually not best for them. (On vacation, do you switch hotels every other day?) Leadership involves unselfish motives. It is honorable to sacrifice in order to give your children a better future, and they will do better because of it (and hopefully, thank you someday).

"Standing tall" includes honesty. In family law cases, the courts require "full and complete disclosure" of all assets and debts to the other spouse. One well-known California case concerns a divorcing wife who concealed from her husband that she had won the California Lottery. The court ruled it as fraud, awarding the husband 100% of the money, thereby sending a strong message of punishment for dishonesty in financial disclosures. So—stand tall and do what is right in your words and deeds.

4. Commitment: Ring Finger

You can probably guess why the ring finger reminded me of the marriage commitment. When we keep our commitments, we demonstrate we can be trusted. If there is any way to save your marriage, please do so! I've had the pleasure of seeing a few couples reconcile during mediation or a collaborative process after they learned better communication skills. (I wish I had more days like that in my week!)

If it's too late to save your marriage, maybe you and your separating partner still want to settle out of court. If you want settlement-minded attorneys for legal advice and creative solutions, consider using the collaborative approach. The most common collaborative model has two attorneys, a neutral financial specialist such as a licensed Certified Public Accountant (CPA) or Certified Divorce Financial Analyst (CDFA), and two coaches—licensed counselors such as Marriage and Family Therapists (MFT) or Licensed Clinical Social Workers (LCSW) to facilitate the best communication. All of these are trained and motivated professionals who focus on amicably reaching results.

Everyone signs a "Collaborative Stipulation," committing to resolving the case without going to court, and identifying the needs, goals and interests of **both parties**. While at first it may seem daunting and expensive to have so many professionals involved, it can result in thousands of dollars of savings over engaging in litigation. Attorney fees for handling subpoenas, depositions, motions, and continuances, plus the expert witness fees (like custody evaluators or business appraisers) will quickly run up your bill.

Let's say Sarah and Hal own a $700,000 home with $200,000 of equity. Sarah wants to keep the house and buy out Hal's interest. She would like to borrow the $100,000 to give to Hal. Unfortunately, she cannot refinance and remove Hal's name from the mortgage without increasing her monthly payments beyond her budget. A judge's solution is to sell the house and split the net equity.

Using a collaborative approach, Hal and Sarah reveal their mutual goal centering around Sarah keeping the house until their 16-year-old son Tom graduates from high school. The financial professional helps them analyze how they might fairly share any increased equity pending a future sale or buyout, the attorneys create the valid court-approved format, and the coaches help design a parenting plan which emotionally supports Tom's desire to stay in the family home until he goes off to college. The professional team supports the parties as they all work together to create a solution that meets their goal.

5. Strength: Pinky Finger

Your little finger is usually your weakest finger. But did you know that guitarists, violinists, and football players do special exercises to increase its strength? Take steps to build strength in your area of weakness. One spouse may need more financial knowledge, another may need parenting tips. Prepare yourself to take on a role previously held by your spouse.

Look for strength, security and happiness in relationships with others who share your core values. If you have a place of worship or other similar community, connect there. Join an accountability group. You can be someone else's strength and he or she can be yours. (Won't it be great to meet others who have survived similar challenges?) I have received "Thank You" cards from clients who attended Divorce Care or Divorce Recovery workshops to rebuild their emotional strength. Others have called me to report feeling relieved and financially stronger after speaking with tax or investment advisors. Be strong and courageous.

By putting the above five strategies—**Encouragement, Direction, Responsibility, Commitment,** and **Strength**—into action, you can be Happy and Secure through what could otherwise have been a painful divorce. Now that you have your fingers to remind you, don't clench them into a fist holding on to past resentments. Use them for a handshake of agreement and move forward. Then you will successfully finish the journey, weather the storm, survive the roller coaster, and earn a big "high-five."

About Jeanne

Jeanne M. Browne is a family law attorney with a private practice in Santa Rosa and a graduate of Empire Law School. She currently serves as Co-President of the Collaborative Council of the Redwood Empire (CCRE), an organization of attorneys, mental health providers, and financial specialists committed to out-of-court resolution. Jeanne served on the Family Law Committee for the Sonoma County Bar Association and is also a board member of the Sonoma County Legal Services Foundation assisting low income clients. She was honored as a featured Alumni at Empire College's 50th Anniversary Jubilee Celebration in 2011.

Jeanne was on the training team for the Court-Involved Therapists Training (CIT) Program for local mental health professionals. Jeanne also serves as a Settlement Conference Panelist for the Sonoma County Superior Court and is often appointed as Minor's Counsel to be the voice of the children caught in the middle of high-conflict custody matters.

She and her husband, Bill, have been married 32 years and they have two grown daughters. They enjoy hiking, reading, and outdoor adventures with extended family.

Chapter 13

Legal Services Tailored to Unleash Your Business

William F. Fritz, Esq.

Henry, the CEO of a large Bay Area retailer, contacted my business law firm with a real emergency. One of his marketing executives had just delivered my client's marketing plan to a competitor just as it was about to be launched—apparently in return for a job. What had taken my client's marketing team a lot of work over many months could now be copied step by step to capture the very market segment that my client was seeking. Henry was understandably very angry, and wanted to immediately sue both the competitor and the former employee, to teach them a lesson.

I could have brought suit for him, and most likely would have prevailed. But would it have gotten him that extra market segment that he was after? The marketing plan had a limited life. Objectively, the goal was securing that segment of the market, rather than punishing anyone. In our conversation I pointed out that my primary purpose was to provide a benefit for his business, rather than to teach anything to anyone else. The real question was how much of some kind of actual benefit could he realize from his investment in legal fees and costs. This required consideration of the economic costs, in addition to the legal fees.

Without a prior trade secret policy agreed upon by his employees, such a lawsuit might also have the unintended consequence of surprising the remaining marketing executives by uncovering a wide gap between what his company claimed to own, versus what ideas and creativity that his executives might believe to be theirs. Their loyalty, commitment, and creativity might suffer if they felt that they had no 'ownership' of any of their own ideas.

We then discussed some innovative ways that Henry and the company could come out ahead without legal action. Ultimately, Henry decided not to spend the time, energy, and money necessary to proceed against the former employee and the other company. Instead, he shrewdly used the resources his company would have spent on litigation to provide employee bonuses to motivate his executives, to pay for preventative legal costs to agreeably clarify with his remaining marketing team what the company owned, and to be advised of the limits of what his company could do in competing with the competitor. This allowed Henry's company to pull together, within a very short time, an aggressive, new marketing strategy that anticipated the marketing plan that had been misappropriated. Their hard work surprised the competitor with an immediate preemptive (and better!) marketing plan. Since they knew the details of what the competitor had stolen, they were able to anticipate and undermine their competitor's attempts to grab that segment of the market, more effectively and with less cost, than could have been realized solely by relying upon court injunctions and litigation, all with minimal risk of litigation.

Clearly, Henry and his company were the 'winners' here. They avoided the considerable fees and costs of litigation and all the stress and disruptions that come with investigations, depositions, and court proceedings. They improved employee happiness and loyalty and ended up with a marketing plan which surpassed the stolen one. The company actually became stronger and more secure from looking at both litigation and non-litigation options.

When starting law school, my focus had been upon getting justice for my clients solely in the courtroom. It did not take very long, however, for me to discover that being a successful business litigator requires a lot more than that. Over the 25 years that followed, I have developed some principles which have helped me become happier and more secure in my professional and personal life, and which directly benefit my clients.

We all have business relationships, whether we own a business or not. Seldom do all of those relationships go smoothly all of the time. Conflicts or situations where we feel taken advantage of or wronged cannot always be avoided. But they can be either anticipated or dealt with efficiently. Not every conflict has to be fought, even if you are clearly the 'injured party.' Businesses must pick their battles very carefully. This requires objectivity. Even a seasoned attorney knows better than to trust his decisions without independent counsel when he finds himself personally involved in a dispute. Stop and think before you rush into a fight. Be clear about what you need and what it will take to obtain it. Here are some questions you might ask yourself:

- Do I really need to 'win,' or am I fighting just because I'm 'right?'

- What will be the costs—financial as well as in time, energy, stress, and business opportunities I will have to overlook for lack of time or money—not simply to "win," but to realize an actual benefit from those costs?

- What do I really need to be satisfied with the outcome of this situation?

- Is there more than one way to get what I need?

- Can I come up with an innovative way to solve the conflict?

- Is there a way for everyone involved to be satisfied?

- Can I do this by myself or do I need assistance?

- How can I use this experience to strengthen my future business prospects?

I have generally rolled these, and many related questions, into three preliminary points of discussion for every case that I accept. One case involved Ted and Andrew, two partners who left their employer at the request of their employer's customers, who valued the high quality of Ted and Andrew's services, but hated dealing with the prior employer's over-priced and unresponsive bureaucracy.

I first met Ted and Andrew in person at the door of the courtroom about ten minutes before a judge was to decide whether to issue a temporary restraining order against them. Their former employer wanted to shut down their attempts to do business with prior or potential customers, effectively terminating Ted and Andrew's fledgling consulting business before it collected a single dime of income. Whether they could even start their new business hung in the balance. Only hours earlier, I had posed my usual three preliminary points of discussion in an initial phone conversation.

First, I asked them about the product or service that they planned to provide in their new business. What I listened for was their passion for excellence, and what set their product or service apart from the competition. There is little benefit to any client in defending the possibility of providing a mediocre product, or a product that has no real future. An experienced attorney knows the long term value, both to the attorney, and especially to the client, in avoiding legal services that fail to provide a long term benefit to the client. This is true regardless of what the client might be willing to do or pay in the short term. Ted and Andrew literally seemed transformed with excitement when describing what they would do differently and better than their former employer. Their passion sustained their business for the next 20 years after I was able to carry their passion into the courtroom and explain the uniqueness of their proposed services, which helped considerably in defeating the adverse claim for an injunction.

Second, I also asked them for a chronology of events supported by copies of related documents. I asked them to conclude with their three or four greatest needs and goals, in their own words and as specifically as they could describe them. Even with only an hour or two to pull this together, these business owners' written chronology allowed me to quickly and effectively get to the heart of the matter. If a business owner feels that the effort to compile a written chronology is too much trouble, it becomes obvious that I am faced with a client who is not willing to do what it takes to realize aggressive and effective legal services. This kind of client will be very difficult to help, regardless of the merits of their case or the amount of effort that I put into it. For example, Ted and Andrew not only welcomed my effort to immediately review their case in detail, but also delivered an entire box of carefully organized documents tagged for reference to their written chronology. They did this all within two hours after the attempted injunction against them had been defeated in court—and all back in the day before emails and private cloud accounts made this considerably easier to do.

Third, I provided Ted and Andrew with an estimate of the attorney fees required to properly prepare for and present argument at both the initial injunction hearing and at the subsequent preliminary injunction hearing that would likely follow, and that might determine the outcome of their case. It is important to learn at the outset if the client can immediately afford such a cost. There is always the possibility that the attorney fees might be much lower, depending upon the amount of effort expended by the business owner to present the strongest possible case, and depending upon what actually occurs in court. But this cannot be assumed. It is important for a client to candidly disclose what resources are immediately available for legal representation, and to accurately and honestly explain what can be provided in the near future. However, if the business owner argues that the cost estimate is too high, especially when it is obvious that the other side has already incurred several times that estimate, then there is little point in going any further. This is also true when it is clear that the other side has a strong enough, rational business incentive to continue outspending the business owner by several hundred percent. Nor is it a good idea to proceed if the business owner avoids assurances of payment by making dramatic promises of sharing in the future success or hoped for profit of the business.

It is important from the outset to fashion alternatives that are truly affordable for a business, and which will allow the business a reasonable chance of continuing to grow in spite of legal fees and costs. Undertaking only part of the representation until exhausting all immediately available funds generally leaves a client in a worse position than if no representation had occurred at all. Additionally, by eliminating the possibility of any conflict over costs, the crucial two-way communication between attorney and client, that is essential to winning, is preserved.

It seldom benefits either the client or the attorney to undertake a procedure or a case in which there is no hope of having enough resources to see the case through to the end, or at least sufficient resources to complete a key legal procedure.

Ted and Andrew, for example, not only fully explained their financial limitations up front, but then bent over backwards to provide a deposit greater than what I had estimated. Their clear determination to defeat the claims against their start-up business proved to be not only very strong, but also made a huge impact upon the opposing side. Although the other side had far greater resources to spend, they did not see the same value in doing so as Ted and Andrew had demonstrated from the start. Between the early loss in court and the visible determination of Ted and Andrew to invest in substantial legal procedures in order to win, the other side soon ceased to see any actual net benefit in continuing with the litigation, which led to an early and most agreeable settlement for Ted and Andrew.

Twenty years after I first met Ted and Andrew at the courtroom door, their fledgling consulting business had grown into a highly successful firm that was nationally regarded in their industry. This was in spite of the Great Recession! Like any business, Ted and Andrew's business endured several claims during those intervening twenty years. However, because of how well I knew and worked with them, they came out of each subsequent dispute not only stronger, but more capable of avoiding disputes and lawsuits in the future.

Last year, I completed my many years of working with Ted and Andrew by representing them in a highly lucrative sale of their business. This allowed them to comfortably retire, while continuing to do the kind of work that they each loved to do, but on a far more leisurely and less risky basis. Simply stated, working with business people who truly love what they do is the key to providing quality service and enjoying the kind of client relationships that span my professional life. It is these long term client relationships that are the most mutually rewarding, economically, personally, and professionally.

In short, a business that will not only prevail in litigating disputes, but will actually be strengthened by adversity, is one that is (1) committed to the kind of excellence necessary to be profitable over time, (2) developed by expending the effort required to build agreeable and reliable business relationships, and (3) worth the time, cost, and hard work to defend or preserve. Such a client generally becomes the kind of long term client for whom I can do my best work and do the most good. A law firm run in the same manner becomes a real support for the life and growth of a client's business.

Having a long term relationship with an attorney who knows and cares about your business and its future allows business owners to do what they do best. Knowing that their attorney is prepared to immediately assist when problems arise, after having minimized those problems by making the effort necessary to anticipate and avoid those problems, enables business owners the freedom to build their business, rather than spending their life reacting to one dispute after another, or, still more tragically, failing to develop their business out of fear. Seeing my clients' businesses succeed is clearly one of the most profitable, as well as most personally gratifying experiences for me as an attorney. As much as I might enjoy trial work, winning in the courtroom is seldom sufficient and is rarely the only option for realizing security and happiness for my clients' business ventures. Having an attorney who is focused on freeing you to conduct your business is what makes that security and happiness actually happen.

About William

William Fritz has practiced law for over 26 years. In 1993 he, along with his wife Theresa, started their own law firm, The Fritz Law Offices, in Santa Rosa. His firm covers the legal needs of family businesses and non-profits, including transactional work and contracts, leases, start-ups, and sales; full litigation support, including bench and jury trials and appeals. The firm practices in a variety of particular areas of law, including Business Successor Planning, Unfair Competition, Construction, Real Estate, and Employment Law.

Mr. Fritz is originally from Southern Illinois and received his Bachelor of Arts Degree from the University of Chicago, where he graduated with honors. After a year of graduate business studies at Arizona State University, Mr. Fritz went on to earn his law degree from UCLA School of Law.

Mr. Fritz served on the Board of Directors for the North Bay Regional Center, is past president of the Young Lawyer Association, tutored struggling students at Burbank Elementary School and lectured in business courses at the local junior college, and has served on a variety of boards from a Church vestry to being elected as the President of a large condominium board in Oakland. His professional memberships include the California Bar Association, the Sonoma County Bar Association and the Healdsburg Chamber of Commerce.

Mr. Fritz keeps busy investing time into making sure his firm stays on top of the latest technological advances, all while raising two wonderful daughters who are currently attending Carnegie-Mellon University and Boston University.

Chapter 14

Do What You're Supposed to Do When You're Supposed to Do It — Eric's Story on the Farm

Eric Gullotta, JD, CPA, MS (Tax)

A new client walked into my office in tears. Sadly, this has not been an uncommon occurrence in my career as an estate planning attorney. As with many clients who have lost a loved one, she was in shock. Lisa (not her real name of course) was 72 years old and her husband had just died from a heart attack. Like most spouses, she didn't expect to lose her soul mate so early. She was distraught. Lisa and her husband had a living trust drafted by another attorney, and she had expected that everything they owned would automatically go directly to her. Unfortunately that wasn't the case, and sadly, her story is not unique.

The first question that I asked her was "Do you know what your trust says is supposed to happen now that you've lost your husband?"

She responded "No." She had no idea what her document said. This was not the answer I wanted to hear—but again it is not an uncommon one.

Not only was this widow dealing with the loss of her husband, but also with the uncertainty of her financial future. I could see the panic in her eyes as I read through her existing trust—she literally had no idea what I was going to say, and whether it would be good or bad. Arguably, this is the most vulnerable position you can be in. It involves a major life change, both emotionally and financially, and it usually occurs in your later years when you're feeling the most at risk. You just can't feel safe and secure without knowing what these legal documents say. The good news is that it is never too late to pick up your existing documents, consult with an attorney, learn what they say, and consider whether they need revision or re-drafting.

As we reviewed her documents it turned out that they had certain provisions that were less than optimal. There were steps we could take to minimize the impact, but unfortunately, this would involve more attorney's fees, more uncertainty, and more worries that she didn't need.

It's important that people understand that estate planning documents are more consequential than most typical legal documents. Trusts and wills are not like contracts or premarital agreements because the drafters will not be around to explain to the court what they actually meant if those documents don't work the way intended. In this case, Lisa's husband was not around to let the court know that instead of restricting their assets, he wanted her to have their full use. She was stuck going to court to try to convince a judge of what her deceased husband really meant.

As I worked with Lisa I found that she and her husband had tried to save a few dollars by having their bankruptcy attorney draft their estate planning documents. And although the legal documents were effectual, they were less than optimal. It's important to remember that attorneys, like doctors, have specialties. In a world as complex as ours those specialties are there for a reason. Do you want a knee surgeon performing your brain operation? Me neither.

Understanding Your Documents

An all too common occurrence, whether one is seeking medical or legal advice, is that the patient or client simply and blindly trusts the professional helping them. Of course, professional advice has value and merit but it is also important to understand the advice. This usually involves asking questions.

This isn't always as easy as it sounds because attorneys are paid by the hour. Many clients have expressed to me the frustration of wanting to have a larger role in the creation of their estate planning documents, but at the same time, feeling that the hourly cost of their participation is not justified. The bottom line is that people just need to get over this. What's the point of paying to have your estate planning documents prepared if you don't understand them?

One way to overcome this is to look for estate planning attorneys who offer flat rates. Thankfully, this is becoming more the norm. When you engage an estate planning attorney to prepare your documents on a flat fee basis there is no consequence for asking questions. When clients ask me questions they usually start by saying, "I know this is a stupid question, but…" The truth of the matter is that there are no stupid questions when it comes to estate planning. As I mentioned before, these documents will speak for you when you cannot speak for yourself. They have very serious legal and financial ramifications at either your death or incapacity. Attorneys spend years learning all the legal aspects of these documents, so how could you be expected to have the same level of knowledge after just a few short meetings?

Attorneys can write 'vanilla' estate plans that perhaps could apply to most of us. However, if you're like me, your family is unique and so warrants unique consideration. Yes, attorneys can get to know you pretty well but they will never get to know you as well as you know yourself. In fact, you are the only person qualified to consult with on what's the best plan for you and your family. Not only do attorneys welcome this feedback, we need it. Good estate planning attorneys strive to draft the best documents they can, and that requires your input.

Once you understand your documents, you can feel confident that when the time comes, your plan will meet your needs and the needs of your family. In fact, studies show that having an understood and properly executed estate plan actually helps with the grieving process we go through when we lose someone.

When I receive calls asking for help from clients who have very recently lost loved ones, it is usually because they don't know what their plans say or they don't have plans. They cannot help themselves, because not only are they reeling from the loss of their loved ones but they are also facing the confusion and fear of the future. Those of my clients who have plans that they understand often wait to contact me until some time after they've suffered a loss, because they're confident that the financial and estate planning aspects of their lives are in good shape. This allows them to focus on grieving for their loved ones with family and friends.

When to Prepare Your Documents

I grew up on a farm in Glen Ellen, California, a small town just north of the city of Sonoma. My family had about 30 acres of land. We raised cattle, chickens and horses, and had a two acre garden and a one-half acre vineyard. As a boy, I spent seven days a week tending to the cattle, mending fences, planting, picking, pruning, and just generally helping to keep the farm in good repair. Rain or shine we were always out, making sure the things that had to get done, got done. In fact, it was this time in my life when my father taught me one of my most valuable lessons:

Do what you're supposed to do when you're supposed to do it.

Work doesn't get done unless you do it and do it when you are supposed to. Planning ahead and taking action is key to success on the farm (and in life). Although I didn't value it at the time, I grew to understand and appreciate this simple lesson. Sure, you can mend a broken fence any time, but if the cows are already out then the task is pointless. This is a lesson that I think is lost on many young people today.

Throughout my life I've been inundated with sayings, proverbs and stories—many of which went in one ear and out the other. But as I've progressed through my professional career and personal life, I've found that they are not only accurate but also excellent guiding principles for success and happiness.

Do what you're supposed to do when you're supposed to do it is something that I live by in my office every day. It helps assure that client work is done on time and done properly. As we all know, mistakes happen when things are done at the last minute. Oddly enough, doing what you're supposed to do when you're supposed to do it relates perfectly to estate planning as well. Many clients try to postpone or delay their estate planning, only to be bitten when the day comes that they need it but it is not done.

Failing to prepare your estate plan—not doing what you're supposed to do when you're supposed to do it—can be costly in terms of time, stress, money and your mental health. It is easy for estate planning attorneys to quantify the cost of failing to prepare your estate plan in terms of money. It's easy to compare what it will cost to go through probate proceedings or a guardianship as opposed to preparing a trust, power of attorney and/or an advance health care directive. But it is not easy to quantify the stress and headache that survivors face when a plan is not in place when a loved one dies. Without a plan, the future is uncertain, and that can be very scary for anyone—let alone somebody who has just lost a loved one.

One of my favorite clients, 'Larry', lives by the same motto as do I—probably because he is a retired Army Captain with a similar background to my father. Larry came to see me because he wasn't in good health and wanted to prepare an estate plan. He felt insecure because he wasn't sure where his assets would go if something happened to him, and he certainly wasn't happy about it. Two days after finalizing his estate plan, he suffered a serious yet (thankfully) not fatal stroke. It was Larry's timing and perseverance that allowed his family, despite his stroke, to be secure in Sonoma and as happy as they could be, considering the circumstances. Larry was not like other clients I have who only come to visit me when they are months past their life expectancy due to a terminal illness. They are surely not doing what they are supposed to do when they are supposed to do it.

Then there was 'Jim.' Jim was about 80 years old, and he and his wife had a significant estate composed of real estate, cash, stocks, etc. They had no children, so estate planning was very important for them.

They needed to be sure that their assets would end up where they wanted, and not go to nieces, nephews, and other distant relatives they did not have a strong connection to. For years Jim would come into my office and always say the same thing, "I know I need to do this. I will get to it as soon as I can." (Actually, that's something I hear quite often in my office. Trust me; I realize that there are a lot of other fun ways to spend your money rather than on estate planning documents!) Jim finally came in and got his and his wife's estate plan done. When we were finished signing the documents, he put the pen down, put his hands up in the air and said "I win!" I looked at him and said "What are you talking about?" He said very simply, "I pushed this off as far as I could; I knew I needed to do it and procrastinated, but here I am, and it's done. I did it before I got sick or died."

The truth of the matter is that Jim was right. He did 'win.' He pushed off preparing his documents as far as he could, but eventually got them signed before they were needed. Jim was lucky that he was not like the thousands of others out there who procrastinate but DON'T get their documents done in time. They 'lose,' and leave their families with messes that will likely cost them time, money and heartache. Why push it that far when preparing your estate plan is so important to your peace of mind and your family's wellbeing?

Who Should Help You With Your Documents?

The last point I want to make comes from a question that I get in my office quite often. Many people will ask, "Why can't I just prepare these documents online?" I don't get mad at this question (any more) because it is a valid question. How you spend your money is an important issue to resolve as a family. If money can be saved by preparing an estate plan online, that is something you could consider.

But—the old adage of "you get what you pay for" could not be more true in this situation. First off, online documents do not create a professional relationship that will be necessary as your life progresses and things change. Attorneys get to know you and your family and become more valuable as planners and counselors as they do. Second, online programs don't ask you the important questions that an attorney would and incorporate those into your legal documents. There is a lot of very important back and forth discussion that occurs, as most estate

154

planning solutions are not simple. You just can't get that with the one-way interface found online.

Of course, I could go on and on about why hiring an attorney is better than online estate planning but I will leave you with this: You are going to jump out of an airplane, and you have a choice as to how your parachute is packed. Will you feel safe going online and packing your own parachute based on instructions from the Internet? Or, will you feel that your life and the well being and security of your family is better left in the hands of somebody who has packed thousands of parachutes before yours and knows exactly what he's doing? I think the answer is clear.

We all need estate planning documents, because the sad truth is that we will all pass away at some point. If you're lucky, you will pass quietly in your sleep after a long and happy life. Regardless of the circumstances, having estate planning documents in place is critical not only to your mental health and happiness while you are alive, but also for ensuring that your family will be safe and secure after your death. If you haven't yet made that will or set up a trust, your cows are still in your pasture, but they are eyeing the gap in your fence. And if you die without these important estate documents, your cows will get out and your heirs will probably not be able to round them back up.

Hopefully, you can take away a few useful tidbits from my chapter about the importance of estate planning in building security for you and your family. If you have not done so already, I urge you to make the call to an estate planning attorney to begin the very important process of preparing your documents. If you are in Sonoma County it will be my pleasure to meet with you at my office, get to know you, and discuss your specific estate planning needs.

About Eric

Eric Gullotta is the founder of Gullotta Law Group with office locations in Sonoma and Santa Rosa. He focuses on estate planning, trust administration, and probate. This includes the preparation of estate documents such as trusts, wills, advance healthcare directives and POA. Further practice areas are taxation and business formation.

Eric is a Sonoma County native, born in Petaluma and raised in Sonoma and Glen Ellen. Eric received his bachelor's degree from the University of California at Santa Barbara in economics and accounting. After graduation he worked for a Napa CPA firm while he studied for and passed the CPA exam and then became a licensed CPA in the State of California. Furthering his qualifications and interest in estate work, he earned a master's degree with honors in Taxation from Golden Gate University in San Francisco while working full time at Richard A. Gullotta, CPA, MBA, Inc. Seeing the need for a special combination of education and experience, without taking a summer off, Eric immediately enrolled at Empire College in Santa Rosa, where he received his Juris Doctor, Cum Laude while working and starting a family. After passing the California State Bar, Eric worked for Sonoma County's largest law firm, Perry, Johnson, Anderson, Miller, and Moskowitz. Later Eric opened his own doors to provide competent, concise and friendly estate planning to residents of Sonoma County.

Eric is a member of the State Bar of California and Sonoma County Bar Association, licensed to practice in front of both the U.S. Tax Court and IRS. He is on the Board of Directors of Becoming Independent, a local non-profit that supports men and women living with a variety of disabilities to seek their own paths to personal fulfillment and independence. Eric has served as president of Sonoma Valley Executives, Inc.

Eric also enjoys sharing his ideas and knowledge on Estate Planning and through writing. His book *Did the Government Write Your Will?* is available on www.Amazon.com.

When Eric is not hard at work handling estate planning and probate for his clients, he enjoys spending time with his children and practicing his hobby of digital photography and videography. He also brews his own beer, plays the drums and frequents the golf course every chance he gets.

Chapter 15

Making Dreams Come True

Kay Marquet

I will never forget the memorial service, held in a little white church in Glen Ellen in 2009. People may have thought it typical, no more than just another service for a very old woman. But what wasn't typical was the bright red fire truck parked in front with "Hazel T" painted on the door. The service was for Hazel Todd, who, with her husband Roland, had lived for many years in their farm house in rural Sonoma Valley, where they were active members of their community.

The Todds had inherited wealth from their families and Roland had been a successful diesel engine distributor, and they had accumulated many millions of dollars more than they would need in their lifetimes. So, in 2000, they wanted to plan the philanthropic distribution of their wealth.

Now, you may not have the sizable funds which Hazel and Roland eventually put to work in their community and through their charitable trust. But whether your legacy will be thousands of dollars, or millions of dollars like the Todds, or somewhere in between, it is my hope that the Todd's story and the guiding principles illustrated in this chapter will help you make your own philanthropic dreams come true.

Back in 2000, the Todds knew they wanted to help make their corner of the world a happier and safer place. When their attorney called me to help advise on the structure, and to carry out Hazel and Roland's wishes, I was the President and CEO of Community Foundation Sonoma County (CFSC), an organization which carries out the wishes of donors in the best interest of the community.

We sat at the dining room table in the Todds' farmhouse, and I listened as they told me that they had no children or other family heirs, and so wanted their significant resources to help serve their community. They knew some of the grants they wanted to make, but did not know exactly what they wanted their remaining assets to achieve, or how to go about giving them away.

I asked them about their interests. Hazel admired the work of FISH (Friends in Sonoma Helping), a volunteer group that provides emergency assistance for hungry families and those on the brink of homelessness. Roland was particularly concerned about his rural neighbors. He knew that the first responders of the local fire departments were the lifeline that people depended on for emergency help. As an engineer, he understood the importance of having good modern equipment, and realized that the Sonoma Valley fire departments were small and desperately in need of equipment.

They both wanted to begin charitable giving while they were alive, and also leave an endowment that would serve their community for years to come. They chose to begin with a donation of three pieces of property which were sold to start their fund at CFSC.

One of the most important aspects of my job was making sure that donated funds had the most positive impact possible, so I started with research. I visited fire departments to listen, assess needs, and receive and review requests. I made a recommendation to the Todds, and they chose to make their first donor-advised grants to three fire departments, for the purchase of equipment. The Kenwood, Schell-

Vista and Glen Ellen fire departments each received $300,000. The Glen Ellen Fire Department used its grant, along with $175,000 they raised, to purchase a new fire engine. Hazel and Roland were happy to see what their funds had achieved, and were simultaneously embarrassed and pleased that the truck was named the "Hazel T."

FISH also received a donation through the Todd Fund at the foundation. It was used to provide food for their food pantry, where people could get free groceries so that they would not go hungry. The grant also supported services for people in danger of becoming homeless.

After both Roland and Hazel died, their assets went into a fund that was created to help Sonoma Valley (and other Sonoma County) residents. Services such as medical care, adult education, and employment training were funded to benefit the health, well-being, and security of people in need.

I worked with the Todds and with their estate planning attorney for many years; our relationship continued until their deaths in 2009. Working with estate planning professionals (lawyers, accountants, trust officers, etc.) is an important part of my work. Donors need assistance turning their dreams into practical realities, and professional expertise is needed to draft the necessary legal documents.

I've been helping people make the world a better place for many years. As an experienced philanthropic advisor, I listen, match your wishes to community needs, research nonprofit and other charitable organizations, create giving plans, and make sure that those plans are carried out. You want to feel secure that your charitable donations will be meaningful and important gifts, and will benefit the things you are passionate about. Making that happen is my job and my passion.

I grew up in the Philadelphia area and then moved to central Massachusetts. After many years in church work as a parish worker, volunteer and minister's wife, I directed a volunteer program for a neighborhood center, where I designed, wrote the grant for funding, and ran an arts/education program. Later I became the first CEO of the Greater Worcester Community Foundation, and spent 13 years there, growing the assets and grant making functions. I wanted to use what I had learned to help another area grow its community resources, and interviewed at Community Foundation Sonoma County. I got the job, and within two months of my arrival I knew that Sonoma County would always be my home. I am glad to be "happy and secure in Sonoma County!" After 30 years of heading two community foundations, I now use my skills as a consultant to help people make their charitable dreams come true.

You have worked hard to provide for yourself and your family. You have achieved many of the goals you set, and now it is time to consider what will bring you happiness in the days to come. What legacy will you leave to the local or global community, to your children and to future generations? I can help you draw up an amazing plan that brings a smile to your heart; a personalized plan that benefits the people and the causes that mean most to you. I have demonstrated success on both sides of the philanthropic equation—as a funder and as one seeking funds. My experience lends a perspective that will maximize the success of your legacy and its benefit to the community.

When I meet with new clients, I first want to know what they want their legacy to achieve. I ask them many questions, the same ones you might want to ask yourself if you are considering a donation now or a bequest from your estate:

- What is your passion?
- What gift of money or property can you make which will represent that passion?
- What specific impact do you want your donation or legacy to have?
- How much control do you want to have?
- Do you want to begin giving now or have your estate distributed later?
- Do you want to give a lump sum, distribute individual gifts, or endow a foundation?
- Do you have specific organizations in mind?
- How long do you want your legacy to continue?
- Do you need a third party to guide your giving?

- Are you working with an attorney and/or accountant?

My clients generally have questions too. These are things you should consider as well, whether you are dropping off used household goods at a thrift store or putting a sizable bequest into your will:

- How do I know my donation will be used the way I want it to be?

- Should I start a foundation, a supporting organization, or donate to an existing charity or fund?

- How can I be sure that the charitable organization will use my gift wisely?

- How much money does the organization use to cover costs and overhead?

- Does the organization have an appropriate investment policy?

- Can I be sure that the fund or trustee I choose is trustworthy?

- So many people have requests—how can I decide who needs help more?

- Will the charities in my will still be around in five, ten, or twenty years?

- How can I plan for alternate beneficiary organizations if my choices are no longer viable after my death?

There are many ways to accomplish your goals—through grants, wills, trusts, endowments and foundations. Financial institutions or community foundations can provide donor-advised funds, where you serve as the advisor on grants that are made during your lifetime. You may want to make other plans to be implemented after your lifetime. It will be important to select the most effective tool to meet your specific wishes. Your ideas and dreams should be the nucleus of your plan.

If you have decided that you want to make a donation, either today or after your lifetime, what is your next step? You seek professional advice for many aspects of your life—for example, an accountant for tax preparation or advice, an investment advisor to help protect and grow your wealth, a real estate agent when it's time to buy house, and a lawyer for legal matters. You also need professional help to maximize your charitable gifts now and in the future, to make sure that your assets create the legacy that you want. An estate attorney and a charitable advisor will make sure that you have the plan that you want and the will and trusts to assure that your dreams are realized.

If you want to give general support to established organizations with a successful track record and a plan for the future, you may not need a charitable advisor like me. If, on the other hand, you are not sure about the effectiveness for the long run of the organizations you're considering, or want to accomplish specific goals, I can be of assistance. I will help you through your thought process with the information and research you will need for peace of mind.

Sometimes I work with clients who know exactly what they want to do with their money. Shortly after arriving in Sonoma County, I had a phone call from a San Francisco attorney. He told me about a client in Sonoma County who wanted to help Santa Rosa teens as well as moms in the county with young children. He said the donor needed to remain anonymous and that the bequest might be in the range of $5 million. Drawing on the knowledge I had from my years with the community foundation in Massachusetts, I was able to provide the attorney with the specific language he needed to draft the client's trust. Years later CFSC received the bequest of $16 million from Charles (Chop) DeMeo.

Chop had worked hard all his life: as a teen, to earn money to help support his family; as a young man, to put himself through college and law school; and as an attorney with a successful law practice in Santa Rosa. He eventually became the mayor of Santa Rosa. His hard work paid off, he and his wife, Eileen, were frugal and he invested wisely. By his later years he had over 16 million dollars to use for charitable purposes.

His passion was helping youth as well as needy mothers with young children. His first big dream was to create a place where Santa Rosa teens could gather, as an alternative to the streets. His other desire was to provide services to help at-risk mothers and their children.

Chop's bequest was a game changer for the foundation, catapulting its assets to $23 million almost overnight! We went through quite a process to seek community input. We held three community forums, formed an advisory board, a youth council, and sought letters of advice from the entire community.

One result was the 21,000 square foot Chop's Teen Club in Railroad Square in Santa Rosa. Another result was that his personal residence was given to Catholic Charities and became a transitional home where at-risk mothers and their children could live and receive support services. Other grants were made to organizations to provide supportive services to help people avoid homelessness or recover from it.

Chop did not want to be known as a donor during his lifetime. Urged by his good friend, Henry Trione, to let people know what he intended, he replied, "No, but won't they all be surprised when they learn what I've done!" His legacy is extremely important in the lives of the youth of Santa Rosa and to families in crises county wide. His dreams came to life and they will continue for many years to come.

My clients often want to know how to interest their children in philanthropy. The first generation may have a significant sense of philanthropy that may not be shared by their children or family members. Through a process of education and engagement, I can help potential second and third generation philanthropists look at the needs and opportunities in their community in a new way—their way. Beginning with a donor-advised fund, the children and grandchildren of philanthropists can see how their interests can be met, and how they can identify and help a favorite program or project.

I worked with two children of one of my clients, who became donor advisors for a sizable fund. Their cooperation on the fund seemed to bring a new dimension to their relationship with each other. Although each of the donor's children had his and her own distinct interests, they collaborated and discussed their plans, and usually agreed jointly on the grants to be made. There was a provision for each to make their own grants if they did not agree, but it was never necessary; they always agreed to support the favorite program of the other. The dream of the original donor was realized. The children did become philanthropists.

I can help you achieve this by presenting your younger children with a variety of preselected organizations that will appeal to them. I can help older teens and adult children discover what they are passionate about, research opportunities, arrange site visits, and encourage them to carry on the legacy of giving.

I bring a wealth of experience in philanthropy to help you make your charitable dreams come true. I have successfully helped many people reach their philanthropic goals, drawing on more than 30 years of working in social services, volunteering, being CEO of two community foundations, and as a philanthropic consultant. My company, Kay Marquet Associates, offers consulting services for community, private, and family foundations, estate planning professionals, and community benefit organizations of all types.

Let's talk about your philanthropic dreams, and work together to make them happen. And although there may never be a shiny new red fire truck with your name on it, I will help you to leave your mark in your own way.

About Kay

Kay Marquet is an award-winning CEO, fundraiser and community builder, with more than 30 years' experience in community foundations, private foundations and community benefit organizations. Kay founded Kay Marquet and Associates in 2009 after serving as CEO of Community Foundation Sonoma County for 17 years. Kay Marquet and Associates offers services for Community Foundations, Private or Family Foundations and Community Benefit Organizations of all types.

After leaving the Community Foundation, Kay directed the operation of Chop's Teen Club, as interim executive director for the 21,000 square-foot club for the youth of Santa Rosa (2009-2010). She also produced the Sonoma Paradise Foundation Children's Concert for 1,200 children at the Wells Fargo Center for the Arts.

Currently Kay serves as an Honor Roll Trustee of Scholarship America, a national education service organization. She served nine years on the governing board, co-chaired the Families of Freedom Task Force, serving the dependents of those killed and permanently disabled on 9/11, was treasurer and chair of the investment committee and audit committee (1983-2014). She is currently on the governing board of Bottom Line, headquartered in Boston, MA. Bottom Line helps disadvantaged high school students get into college, graduate and go far in life.

She was previously appointed to the New England Board of Higher Education by Massachusetts Governor Michael Dukakis and to the Massachusetts Community Service commission by Governor William Weld. Kay is a current member of the Santa Rosa Chamber of Commerce and former board member. She received the Sonoma County Gold Award for community service, the Jewel of a Woman Award, and the Sonoma County Jefferson Award for volunteer service.

Kay has enjoyed living in Sonoma County for 22 years. She has three children and four grandchildren who all get together in July each year on Cape Cod. She is a regular at the Farmer's Market each Saturday for produce and flowers which she enjoys arranging for her home and for others. Kay enjoys travel, wine tasting, entertaining friends and visitors from out of town, concerts and any excuse to enjoy more of Sonoma County.

Chapter 16

How to Be Happy Buying and Selling Your Home in Sonoma County

Susan Pack

'**M**ark and Marie,' a combination of past clients of my real estate business, were not happy. I was meeting them for the first time and was amazed at the flow of angry words. "At first we couldn't even get a real estate agent to call us back. I guess we didn't know the magic words we needed to get a response. We wanted to sell our house and buy a bigger one before the baby came, but you can see that that didn't happen." Their three month-old baby, Teresa, was asleep in her carrier beside the desk.

"We finally found an agent, and she finally put the house on the market, but we didn't get any offers. We don't think anyone even looked at our house. We never saw the agent, she never returned our calls, and she didn't seem to be doing anything to help us. We have been fed up and frustrated for months, but had to wait for the contract to expire. Now you have been recommended to us—can <u>you</u> help us? Can we trust you? What makes you any different from the last agent?"

When I answer or return phone calls or emails I often hear "WOW, I can't believe you answered the phone!" or "You're the first agent who has called me back!" or "I just emailed you and you contacted me immediately—great!" Many businesses have lost sight of the fact that service and responsiveness are extremely important. This used to be the norm, but no longer. Now when you respond quickly or give good service, it sets you apart and shows that you care!

When I retired from 35 plus years in advertising and marketing, I thought I was ready to be done working. I thought I'd travel and see the world, spend more time with my family and grandchildren, and just enjoy retired life. But there was a surprise in store for me—I decided to become a real estate agent! My partner, Mel Gilson, a real estate broker, convinced me that real estate would be perfect for me. It would give me a new purpose and keep me involved and challenged, but best of all, I would work with people, helping them with one of the most important decisions of their lives—buying a home. And not just any home, but one in spectacular Sonoma County with its rolling hills, open spaces, lush vineyards and great communities. It's been one of the best decisions I've made in my professional life.

Mel and I have built our business, Gilson Real Estate, on the principles of good service and responsiveness to our clients. When they call, we answer, and when they write, we respond immediately. No client is too small for us. We treat all our clients equally, whether they buy a ten thousand dollar mobile home or a ten million dollar estate. Everyone gets the same excellent service—professional, responsive, and personal.

In my advertising and marketing career I always put my clients first. In my last position, I had clients who stayed with me for over 18 years because they knew I cared about their businesses. I cared about getting them the best possible results and value for their money, and I gave them the service they wanted. I have brought this philosophy to my real estate business. It's important to me that my clients get an agent who cares, who is honest, and who has their best interests at heart. I do my best to be that agent!

When it's time to purchase a home, there are many things to think about and do to ensure that the experience will be a happy one. The process can be daunting, and the questions can seem endless: Where do I start? How can I feel secure that everything will turn out well? How do I find an agent? What kind of home do I want and where do I want to live? What can I afford and how will I pay for it? Are there costs beyond the asking price? How does my credit impact my ability to get a loan? What about selling my current home—what is it worth, how do I put it on the market, and how long will it take? And most importantly, who can answer my questions and help me get through this?

I hope you know the answer to that last question! An excellent real estate agent, who has <u>your</u> best interests at heart! Here are some helpful hints and items to review before you make an appointment with an agent.

How do I find a good agent who will be right for me?

Ask your friends, co-workers, or neighbors for referrals. Drop into a real estate office and see how you are treated. Check with the Better Business Bureau for complaints against the office or agent, or if you're doing this on-line, check to see how many reviews they have and what those reviews say. Before sitting down with a prospective agent, create a list of questions to ask.

Here are a few suggestions:

Are you familiar with today's technologies?

- Can you do cost analyses on homes we are interested in?

- Are you familiar with the various neighborhoods in the cities or counties you sell in?

- Can you tell me about schools in the areas I'm interested in and what their ratings are?

- Are you reachable by phone when I have questions?

- Will you make sure that I understand all fees and costs before the closing?

You will have other questions which are specific to your family's needs. Write them down ahead of time and then do your interviews. Ask to see testimonials. Then choose the agent that you feel the most comfortable with. The most successful and happy buyers are those who find an agent they like to work with and then stick with that agent. If you find later that your agent is not giving you the service or attention you expect, do not hesitate to find another agent who will meet your needs.

What kind of a house should I buy and where?

Do you want a 3 bedroom 2 bath home with a large backyard in a new neighborhood, a smaller house with less yard to keep up, or do you want a condo or townhouse with a small patio area and no yard work at all? If you have school-aged children, are you interested in a particular school district? How important is public transportation to you? Do you want to be able to walk to work or shopping?

What can I afford? Should I pay cash or finance?

If you are going to be paying cash, you will need to show proof of funds, and if you are going to finance, you will need to have a pre-approval letter from a bank or a mortgage broker. Before you start looking at houses, it is very important to contact a bank or mortgage broker to see what you can afford to offer. Some of the things which can influence the type and amount of loan you can get are your credit score, your debt-to-income ratio (which usually cannot be more than 40-45% of your income), and your available down payment.

How will taxes and insurance costs impact my mortgage?

When planning to buy a house, most people look at their budget and calculate what they can afford. Often overlooked, however, are costs such as taxes, homeowner's insurance (which may include insurance for earthquakes and floods), and private mortgage insurance. These can increase your final payment, which will reduce the amount you can spend on a home. For example, for every hundred dollars you spend in taxes, insurance or HOA (Homeowner's Association fees), your buying power will be reduced by approximately $20,000. If you have questions and want to see the math, contact your real estate agent.

What about my credit score? What should it be to get a good loan?

Your score should be at 620 or above. You may be able to obtain a loan with a lower score, but will pay a higher interest rate for the money. If you want to improve your credit score, you may need to contact a credit repair company.

I want to sell my house, but how do I know how much it is worth?

You will need to have a real estate agent visit your home, to look at your house and the neighborhood. A good agent will look at the size and condition of your home, the number of nearby homes sold in the last six months, the size of the lot, the demand in the neighborhood and the market in general and finally, any obvious repairs which are needed. Your agent will then do comparisons of recent sales of homes within about two miles of your house. With that information, and drawing on his or her personal knowledge and local experience, your agent will be confident about your asking price.

How do I put my house on the market?

Once the market value of your home has been established, and an asking price has been set, you will sign a six month listing agreement. Your agent may point out cleaning, minor repairs, painting or landscaping projects which will help your house present well. The agent may also suggest decluttering and staging the rooms to make your home feel larger, and to help potential buyers be able to imagine themselves living there. A great agent will also make sure that quality photos are taken, and will write a good description of the property, which will be entered into the Multiple Listing Service (MLS) for the county where you live. Your agent should check in with you weekly, letting you know if there has been any action from buyers. If the action is none to minimal, your agent should sit down with you to re-evaluate the plan.

How long will it take to sell my home?

Most sellers ask this question. The answer will usually be "It depends." Some factors which influence the answer are the supply of and demand for homes in your area, the asking price, and of course, location, location, location! Also, is your agent knowledgeable, experienced, enthusiastic, and marketing to the correct demographic? All of these questions will have an impact on how long it will take to sell your home. Your agent should be able to give you an idea of how long it will take in the current market.

For most homeowners, their home is their castle, their sanctuary, and their private personal space. It's the place where they feel secure and safe. For most people, their home will be the most valuable thing they will ever own, and it can be a source of financial security when they get ready to retire. I love helping all sorts of people buy and sell their homes. It has given me great rewards and great pleasure to know that I have been an important part of one of the biggest decisions they make.

All my clients know that I care first and foremost about them and their needs. To illustrate, I'd like to tell you about 'Bob and Nancy,' a couple I worked with when I first started in this business. This very nice but nervous couple had been trying to contact agents through on-line real estate sites and weren't getting any responses. I suspected that they weren't getting call-backs from agents because they were requesting information about mobile homes. Most agents consider mobile home sales to be such small sales, with such small commissions, that they are not worth the effort. I don't think that way.

They had sent a request through the on-line real estate site, Zillow.com, where I advertise. I responded to their request by telephone as soon as I saw it, and with surprise and relief Nancy said, "You are the first agent who has called us back. We've been trying for days to get someone to call us and were beginning to think that no one cared." "I care," I told her. We talked a bit and I introduced myself and our company and what I could do to help them.

At our first meeting, Nancy said they had received a large settlement and wanted to buy their first home, probably a mobile home. I asked them a lot of questions: Where were they interested in living? How much could they afford to spend? How large of a home and yard did they want? Would they be paying cash or financing?

In order to finance a mobile home, it must have been manufactured after 1977. A mobile home is considered to be personal property (since it can be moved), and so you cannot get a real estate loan from a bank. You must get a loan from an investor instead.

Bob and Nancy said they wanted to pay cash and wanted to buy a 2 bedroom 2 bath mobile home with a small garden, located in a specific area of the county. I started searching and found some homes for them to look at. I set up viewing times and took them to see the properties. They saw one they loved that fit their needs perfectly. "This is the house we want to put an offer on!" they told me, and so we did.

When purchasing a mobile home, you must be pre-approved by the mobile home park where the home is (or will be) located. The parks require that you earn an income of at least 3 times the amount of the space rent. (Space rent is what the park charges you to have the mobile home sitting on the piece of property.) Your credit must be good and your income-to-debt ratio must be no more than 40-45%.

We immediately got an application from the park and I submitted their offer. Two days later the offer was accepted and they received park approval. We closed 30 days after the acceptance of the offer, and Bob and Nancy were the owners of their first home.

After the closing, I handed them the keys to their home. They looked happily around and said to me, with tears in their eyes, "We never thought we would ever have anything so GRAND! Thank you for helping us find our dream home!" I walked away from this sale feeling proud and incredibly touched.

We all have different dreams about what we want in a home, but our feelings about our homes are the same. I will never forget the look of pride and ownership Bob and Nancy had when they were finally able to buy their dream home.

I have traveled to many other countries, and though they have their wonderful places, when I come back home to Sonoma County I realize how fortunate I am to live in this beautiful area. I love the climate and being able to spend time in the interesting and charming towns and cities of our county. We are so central to everything—the coast, the mountains, and the unique and exciting city of San Francisco.

Sonoma County is a place where I have felt happy and secure for many years. I look forward to continuing to help people have happy and satisfying experiences buying and selling their homes here. I get excited that they will be living in this wonderful county with great homes, great neighborhoods, good schools, beautiful parks and much more. If you are looking for a real estate agent who is experienced, knowledgeable, and caring; who answers phone calls quickly and is easy to get a hold of; and who truly wants to help you enjoy the happiness and security of owning a home in Sonoma County, call me.

About Susan

Susan Pack is a licensed real estate agent and a partner in Gilson Real Estate in Santa Rosa, California. Mel Gilson founded Gilson Real Estate in 2004, and Susan joined the company as a partner in 2012. They currently retain a total of five agents.

Susan retired after 35+ years of working in marketing and advertising. For the last 19 of those years, Susan worked for Valpak, one of the leading direct marketing companies in North America and a part of the Cox Media Group, where she was one of the top sales people in her office. Susan realized she wasn't ready to stop working and after looking into several opportunities, she found that real estate was a natural fit. Meeting and helping people make one of the biggest decisions of their lives, buying or selling a home, has been incredibly rewarding. Good customer service and timely communication is the cornerstone of her business.

For over 20 years Susan has resided in Santa Rosa where she lives with Mel, their two cats and one dog. Her two children and their respective spouses live close by and Susan enjoys being a Nana to her five grandchildren. Besides her passion for travel, Susan enjoys reading, running, family dinners, great friends, and just living life.

Chapter 17

Insuring Your Health and Security

Teri Sackett

Our insurance agency sells security and happiness…

Craig owned a small auto repair shop in Rohnert Park. He was 34 years old, a little overweight but in overall good health when he responded to our direct mail flyer. He was curious as to the costs associated with purchasing a group medical plan for himself and his two employees although he rarely visited a doctor and was not convinced he needed the protection.

We met and he decided begrudgingly to purchase not only a group policy for medical but also an individual life insurance policy on himself since he was newly engaged to be married.

Seemed like I heard Craig's grumblings about the high costs of his useless insurance most months until the phone calls suddenly stopped. After several months his wife called. Craig had had a serious heart attack and had been hospitalized for an extended amount of time because of an undetected heart condition. His new bride wanted to verify that his insurance was intact since the bills from his hospital stay were enormous.

Sadly, Craig died shortly after his wife's call, but thankfully all except $500 was covered through the medical plan he had purchased. And his young pregnant widow received the life insurance proceeds, which greatly improved her financial security.

We hear all too often how insurance is unnecessary, a scam or too expensive to purchase. But when you, or your employee, are struck with a sudden illness or accident, financial and emotional security can be shattered quickly.

I had not originally planned to work in the field of insurance, but in 1979 my father had just begun marketing a new type of group health insurance and invited me to join his business. I was pregnant with my first child, living with my husband in Antioch. Since my dad lived in Sonoma County, my husband and I sold our home in Antioch, I quit my job and we moved to Santa Rosa to begin a new journey.

But within 3 months our plans had changed. My father accepted a position with a large insurance company located in Iowa, and I was on my own. No experience, no contacts, no income, a new baby and...scared.

I found a specialist in group health insurance and attached myself to his agency, barraging them with questions, learning anything and everything about small group health insurance. I made cold calls (not a lot of fun!) and put together a direct mail program where my response level was around 6%. To this day I still have clients from those early contacts. I was pleasantly surprised by how friendly and amicable owners of small businesses were.

The only business plan I had at first was to sell and make money. But I soon discovered I needed to set attainable goals and to do the best job possible for my current clients in order to gain their praise and referrals. My goal was not about making money as much as being honest and becoming an expert. The money was not the aim but rather the aftermath of my expertise. (That was a good thing, because in the first 5 months I received commission checks totaling $58! Woo Hoo!)

At one point in my career helping businesses provide health insurance for their employees, I worked from a cramped area in my garage, while still trying to come off as a corporate professional. One memory which always brings a smile to my face was when I was speaking with a new client on the phone and a gust of wind blew open both doors in my "office." In came one of my chickens, chased by my cat, with my collie following in full barking mode. The noise was horrific and at first I was appalled that my client could hear the unprofessional mess. But at that moment I gave up the corporate charade and began to laugh at the hilarious situation. (My very professional client laughed as well.) I learned at that point to be who I am. My clients seem to appreciate how very human their insurance broker is. They relate better with someone real rather than a façade.

Today our agency, with its "corporate" headquarters in my big red barn in the country, is still small, with only four of us. Having competent, reliable, honest, caring employees enhances our agency, and each of us complements the others. For example, I have found that I enjoy spending time with clients more than handling the administrative details, and that makes my assistant, Lorry, indispensable in the agency, since Lorry thrives on detail.

There are three principles that our agency operates by that I believe set us apart from our competitors.

First, we keep the explanations as simple as possible. While we do, of course, provide all the many pages of legal paperwork, we have found that the majority of employers and their employees just want us to go over the basics in our explanations of employee benefits.

Through the years premiums have risen dramatically, and consequently, employers are usually most concerned with the bottom line. (Health insurance is now the second highest expenditure most employers face after payroll.) In the past, employers would have human resource directors to review and decide on benefits. Now, this chore often falls to the company president or owner.

When conducting employee meetings in order to explain benefits, it is extremely important to show employees the true cost of the insurance premium (before the employers' contribution) so they may thank their employers for their generosity. I found that the majority of workers have no idea why benefits were decreasing and why their contribution toward the insurance continued to rise.

Secondly, we now choose to deal only with positive, happy clients. In the past I took on any client, even the unhappy, miserable and demanding ones. But I soon found that these people not only stressed themselves but my staff and me as well. (It's not a good sign when your staff member sees caller ID and lets out a groan.) I believe this actually helps us care about our clients—because we like them! And they are generally so pleasant that my staff genuinely wants to go out of the way to give excellent service.

Finally the **third** area that sets us apart is good old-fashioned service. We have real people answer the phones—nothing automated, no frustrating prompts. We return phone messages and answer emails promptly. We also check up on our clients at least every quarter to make sure they do not have any questions about claims or billing, or any confusion about the many notices they receive from insurance companies regarding the Affordable Care Act. We listen to our clients (and their employees) so that everyone's insurance needs are met.

We do our best to be an outstanding agency, and work hard to implement our three main principles.

Here are four key issues for you to think about before meeting with an insurance agent to address your business insurance needs.

First, decide what you as an employer are attempting to accomplish. Do you want the richest benefits, with the least out-of-pocket expenses for your employees, in order to retain key workers? Are you trying to match your competitors' benefits? Or are you looking for catastrophic coverage at a minimal cost?

A few years ago Tom, a long-time small business owner in Santa Rosa, acquired a number of employees by purchasing many of his competitors' businesses. He went from having eight employees whom he knew quite well to over 100 employees—most of whom he had never met. Most of the small companies he acquired had fairly rich benefit packages with very low co-pays and minimum expense to the employees.

Tom looked at setting up an HRA (health reimbursement arrangement) when the concept was quite new and confusing. But the employees were in a state of flux and confusion over losing their previous employers. Seeing what they perceived as their benefits becoming sparse, many became disgruntled and quit their jobs because of the bare bones benefit package Tom offered. They did not consider this to be a "benefit." And the situation did not benefit Tom, either!

Second, know your options. There are many creative ways in which to get affordable health insurance and continue protecting your employees' peace of mind. Here are several.

Health Savings Accounts (HSA) became extremely popular a few years ago. These are accounts set up for individual employees in order to pay for medical costs that are not covered on their insurance plans, or to help offset the expenses incurred toward the deductibles.

In order to open a Health Savings Account the employee must be enrolled in a particular HSA compatible health insurance policy. These are insurance plans where all medical costs apply toward a high deductible. The only type of service which is covered before the deductible is met is for preventative care such as mammograms, pap smears, immunizations, well-baby care, and annual physicals. All other care such as office visits, x-rays, prescription drugs, and hospitalizations will apply toward the deductible before the insurance begins paying a benefit.

The advantage of purchasing the HSA compatible insurance plan along with a Health Savings Account is the cost savings for the actual insurance. Many employers would then opt to fund the employees' HSA given the savings in premiums. This is also a federal tax deduction for the employer.

The disadvantage to the employer was the money contributed to an employee's HSA was immediately the employee's money since it is an individual account. The employer has no access nor control over the money, basically making it a gift. Obviously, this can become problematic with a high turn-over business.

When first offered, these were worthwhile options to traditional rich insurance plans. However now that so many employers have stripped down their benefits the HSA option isn't quite as appealing since the premium savings is not as great in comparison to their less rich benefits.

Now, with the Affordable Care Act, many employers are taking advantage of the public exchange known as the <u>Covered California SHOP</u> program. This option is quite attractive for employers with fewer than 25 employees whose average annual income does not exceed $50,000, since employers may qualify for tax credits for their portion of the premiums.

There are also <u>private exchanges</u> in California that are gaining in popularity. Traditionally, insurance companies have "participation requirements". This means that if two insurance companies are being offered to a small business, one insurance company may require 75% of the eligible employees to enroll in their plan. It is difficult to manage those percentages when you offer two carriers but must encourage one carrier over the other to meet participation.

Because of these restrictions, private exchanges have loosened those requirements. In a private exchange employees may choose any carrier from an extensive list of companies with different networks of doctors and hospitals but with billing in one central location. This is an ideal situation when employees want to be able to choose a specific provider.

<u>Health Reimbursement Arrangements</u> (HRA) have been fine-tuned enough through the years to be a viable alternative for employers. Unlike the HSA plans, HRAs are funded solely by the employer. After claims are paid for employees, any remaining dollars are the employer's. There can be considerable cost savings using this vehicle, particularly for groups with few health care expenses. Traditionally only 5% of any group actually uses the full benefit offered through the employer's health insurance.

Third, think about how you can lower health insurance costs for your business. Wellness programs, especially in the large group market, can be very effective. Promoting healthy lifestyles can potentially lower medical claims within a business and possibly decrease premiums. And there are added bonuses in improving employees' health—less absenteeism, less depression, less stress and happier and more productive employees. And these all add up to a healthier business for you!

Fourth (and this is the most important suggestion in shopping for your employee benefits), is to find a competent insurance broker whom you trust. The complexities of the implementation of the Affordable Care Act make it imperative to work with a competent, educated broker, one who keeps up on the ever-changing rules and regulations and continues to educate employers and employees alike. (You will be glad to know we are lucky enough to have many extremely competent caring brokers in Sonoma County!)

These are some basic issues to think about to ensure that you will have the insurance you need to keep your business and its employees happy and secure. In addition, there are other kinds of insurance which could have a big impact on your personal happiness and security.

As we age we are constantly reminded of our own mortality and how fragile our health can be, but losing the ability to work is seldom addressed. Earning an income is your biggest asset and often is not insured. Long Term Disability Insurance is often overlooked, yet it is one of the most important areas where you need protection. Most people do not have sufficient savings to last two months, let alone a long term disability.

Another area that many people overlook is Long Term Care Insurance. No one wants to think of themselves in a nursing home, and the costs are exorbitant if that occurs. Most long term care policies have home health care included, which is what most people would prefer. We get many calls from people whose parents or grandparents had to be placed in a care facility. Without long term care insurance, these individuals found themselves destitute and in the Medi-Cal system. No one wants that to happen or to have to rely on family members to care for them.

Your Life Insurance should also be reviewed as your needs change. Many young families are under-insured, with no security for a surviving spouse or children, while many older clients are over-insured since all their once-dependent children are out of college and on their own.

In this day and age of health care reform (and with the ongoing changes to this very complex law), it is a challenge to educate ourselves and our clients. Much frustration and a lot of hair pulling happened during the first onslaught of panic in 2013, in particular. But we remain on course in helping our clients gain some happiness and security in their health care insurance needs.

We love living in this phenomenal Sonoma County, working in our beautiful red barn and sharing our lives and passion with our many friends and clients. So come take a drive in the country and visit us. We will welcome you with open arms. Let our friendly, competent staff help you with your insurance needs and experience country living at its finest...and don't be surprised if you see a chicken or two.

About Teri

Teri Sackett is the founder and owner of Sackett & Associates Insurance Services offering individual and group insurance. Teri began her independent agency in 1979 and from day one was committed to the principles of service, integrity and professionalism while providing clients with the highest quality of service. Operating out of a beautiful quaint red barn in west Sonoma County, Teri is proud of her client-centered approach that is at the heart of her company's business philosophy.

Originally from Orange County, Teri attended Cal Poly Pomona and California State University at Fullerton. Teri has a background in newspaper advertising, but switched gears and has developed a successful and rewarding insurance agency and now enjoys helping her clients/friends with all their insurance needs.

A charter member of the North Coast Association of Underwriters she is a past board member and is currently enjoying many hours of continuing education with the ever-changing Affordable Care Act provisions and law in order to educate her group and individual clients.

In her spare time, Teri enjoys travel, photography, gardening, hiking and of course spending time with family and friends (especially her two young grandchildren!)

Client Quotes About Being Happy & Secure in Sonoma County

"Being happy and secure in Sonoma County means enjoying the fruits of our labor in retirement. Happiness is being able to serve the needs of others when it is within the power of your hand to do so. Much of my happiness comes from time spent with my wife, grandkids, family and friends. Jesus Christ has richly blessed us, living in a county with so much. I grew up with a quote from my Uncle Mel: 'Work hard but enjoy every day.'"

— Ron Campbell

"Being happy and secure in Sonoma County to me means having a beautiful wife who has loved me and lived with me here in lovely Sonoma County for the past 23 years and there is no question in my mind that our love will continue to grow as we live the next 23 or more years together."

— Jeff Sacher

"Key to us is: A Significant Other, someone you love and love to spend time with. Laughing and hugging—cherishing each other into old age. Good health, giving you the ability to maintain intellectual curiosity, travel, volunteer and stay socially active. Getting up each morning and embracing the beauty of the environment that surrounds us. Of course, you need enough money and you need to take good care of it."

— Joe & Alanna Brogan

"Being happy and secure in Sonoma County means knowing my neighborhood and my town and loving it; having at least one child within easy driving distance, and knowing Monty is looking out for my investments. Security also involves my very competent husband, who in spite of having too much "stuff" around the house, is very easy to live with and an excellent handyman!"

— Joanne Dranginis

"My 'happiness' with living in Sonoma County is much more than financial 'safety.' I have a strong trust that Monty and Company are working in my best interest and will honor my choices in how I want my financial resources managed. My happiness involves my faith family, my work world, the richness of natural beauty, cultural opportunities and the climate. Thank you for all that you do to keep me financially informed. I appreciate all the educational opportunities you provide."

— Penny Hunt

"For me, being happy and secure means enjoying time with the love of my life and our black lab, working hard towards building a financially stable and fun future together, exploring the beautiful parks and gems of the area, and traveling—yet always being happy to return home to beautiful Sonoma County."

— Danielle Putonen

"To me, being happy means security. To be happy, life does not need to be a rip-roar of thrilling excitement at all times, but rather a relaxed joyful peacefulness that I obtain through having and maintaining security. Security in financial terms and security in sustaining meaningful relations with those I care about. For me the two coexist; without one I cannot have the other."

— Kelly Mills

"Moving to Santa Rosa to be closer to my daughters and grandchildren has brought me immeasurable happiness. It is pure icing on the cake to live in such an incredibly beautiful natural setting. Having the tools to manage my financial resources provides me with a sense of security and peace of mind which enables me to more fully enjoy the multitude of benefits of living in Sonoma County."

— Kathie Klein

"As I write this, I am traveling down the Danube—in style and great contentment—in a lovely Viking longboat, drinking in the breathtaking sights, seeing history at every stop, and making new friends and acquaintances. Underlying this experience is the security of knowing that because of our planning sessions with Monty— along with his brilliant team of professionals—we can afford and have said 'yes' to this fabulous opportunity! We are grateful to live in our beautiful 'spot' of the world."

— Valerie Brophy

"Being happy and secure in Sonoma County means having a steady retirement income, good health and being active, both physically and mentally. My happiness also includes spending quality time with family and friends and enjoying the beauty of the great outdoors."

— Barbara Shaw

"Happiness and security all comes down to one thing—my family. I love living close to part of my family; I only wish my son and his family lived closer. But at least I am lucky enough to afford a visit to their home fairly often. Being financially secure in my retirement years is a big relief and has helped to ensure that I can continue to see my loved ones when I want. It also makes me feel very content knowing I have provided for them by having a formal will and long term health care so as to not be a burden in my later years. Oh, and let's not forget that being a grandmother is one of my greatest joys in life!"

— Nancy Roberts

"As a former self-employed senior citizen, now pushing ninety, I have seen the importance of transferring some of my vital responsibilities to others such as family and friends. Since a few of us have different abilities, even we know when it is wise to turn to efficient, caring professionals who have earned our trust. Our team at Montgomery Taylor's office seems to be one we can afford to see as often as needed and above all, you are close to home. This offers peace of mind which to me is foremost for a secure and happy retirement."

— Denis Kliene

"Happy and Secure in Sonoma County means to me that I have adequate funds for retirement, a hobby or two, my family and friends in the area, intellectual challenge via classes or The Sonoma County Genealogical Society and time to visit the gorgeous places in our county like Bodega Bay. Luther Burbank was right when he called Sonoma County, "God's chosen place on all the earth." We have such beauty here with the sea, the vineyards, the redwoods and agriculture. My happiness also includes my beloved German Short-Haired Pointer dog, Cambridge (aka "Goober") and the exercise and companionship he provides. I also find time to pray and journal everyday to count my blessings as a retired teacher and practicing Grandma/Great-grandma."

— **Linda Beltz**

SECTION III

FINANCIAL INDEPENDENCE RESOURCES

Introduction to Financial Independence Resources

P eople seeking happiness and security need an abundance of two things: Resources and Resourcefulness.

Resourcefulness is the ability to take whatever resources you have or can obtain and turn them into what you want. To invent, innovate, and implement. To overcome obstacles and adversity. To get things done.

To some extent, you need resources to be resourceful. Even a Boy Scout needs two dry sticks and some how-to information in order to start a fire.

I have been an aggressive gatherer of information my entire life. Whenever confronted with a new opportunity or a problem, my first response is to gather information, and my second is to find experts. I want to know as much as I can before I act. That doesn't mean paralysis of analysis or endless procrastination. Fortunately, there is a wealth of information readily available on just about any subject.

I have also been an avid reader all my life. I read autobiographies and biographies of successful people for insight, ideas, inspiration, and encouragement. I read business books, self-improvement books, and how-to books in every area of interest. I am always surprised when I encounter individuals who don't read!

In this section, I've provided a list of suggested reading on building financial security. It is by no means an exhaustive or complete list, and for the sake of brevity, it omits many books, periodicals, and newsletters I regularly read or own and reread from time to time. I mean no disrespect to any author whose works I've omitted. I've tried to build more of a starter list here. Also in this section, I've listed people I think you need to "meet," if not in person, then through their web sites, newsletters, seminars, books, or other resources. Again, I've omitted many names that would make a more complete and exhaustive list, with no disrespect or slight intended. Also in this section is contact information for just about everyone mentioned in the book.

First, though, I want to share with you something a mentor shared with me when I was young and getting started in business. He gave me a record (yes, an actual 45 rpm vinyl record) of Earl Nightingale's *The Strangest Secret,* a 1956 Gold Record with plenty of history. At the time, I didn't know who Earl Nightingale was or why I should bother listening to the record. I'm glad I did!

Earl Nightingale was an American motivational speaker and author, known as the "Dean of Personal Development." In the early 1950s he was the voice of Sky King, the hero of a radio adventure series, and was a WGN radio show host from 1950 to 1956. Earl Nightingale was in the practice of giving his co-workers a pep talk once a week. One time he was planning a trip and knew he would be away from the office, so he prerecorded his pep talk so his associates could get their weekly message. This 30-minute message was deemed so powerful that in 1956 "The Strangest Secret" was produced for sale and went on to sell over a million copies.

To me, Mr. Nightingale's message was a motivating shot in the arm, just what this young man needed. And let me say this: If you have never heard it, or haven't listened to it recently, go listen to it now. It is easy to find...you can get to a free online recording by doing a Google search.

I recently attended a funeral where the pastor made a comment about gravestone dates. He said that the little <u>dash,</u> between the date we're born and the date we die, represents our life. But that little dash is really our big life story and it lives on beyond our days. Right now, we're writing our story in the way we live our life, express love, smile and laugh, show our gratitude....and in so many other ways. Later, our story will continue in the legacy we leave behind. Let's write something wonderful!

I keep a list of people I intend to meet, the next books I will read, and the information I need and am seeking. You should, too. Hopefully, the information on the following pages will help.

Books to Read/People to Meet for Financial Independence Development

Money/Wealth

Whatever Happened to Penny Candy? by Richard J. Maybury. This small book is the economic lesson we should have had in grade school but didn't. It's not too late to read it! It is a remarkably easy and fun (Really!) explanation of investment cycles, velocity, business cycles, recessions, inflation, money demand and more. The author writes it as a series of letters to his young nephew, in order to make this topic very readable. Contact: www.chaostan.com

The Money Mystery by Richard J. Maybury. Velocity, the hidden force affecting your business, career and investments, and what you can do about it. During the 1980s, the velocity of circulation of the dollar became erratic; now the whole country is affected. Topics include why Federal Reserve officials remain so afraid of inflation, the financial hair-trigger, and precautions you should take. Not one analyst in a thousand realizes what velocity is doing to us, but you will. Contact: www.chaostan.com

The Clipper Ship Strategy by Richard J. Maybury. Conventional wisdom says that when the government expands the money supply, money descends on the economy in a uniform blanket. This is wrong; money is injected into specific locations causing hot spots or "cones," such as the tech bubble of the 1990's. Mr. Maybury explains his system for tracking and profiting from the cones. Contact: www.chaostan.com

The Millionaire Next Door by Thomas Stanley. This is an inside peek at how millionaires, especially millionaire business owners, actually make, preserve, invest, and spend their money, think about money, and grow wealth. Your money education isn't complete without studying this book and Stanley's other works. Contact: www.thomasjstanley.com

Think and Grow Rich by Napoleon Hill. This is about the success secrets of hundreds of American's most successful men (not many female tycoons in the 1930s when this was written). Hill defined the success philosophy that just about all subsequent authors, lecturers, and coaches in the field have studied. In one survey, more CEOs ranked *Think and Grow Rich* as the most influential book they'd ever read, other than the Bible. Contact: www.thinkandgrowrich.com.

The Richest Man in Babylon by George S. Clason. Acclaimed as the greatest of all inspirational works on the subject of thrift and financial planning, this book presents a sure path to prosperity and happiness. It offers an understanding of—and a solution to—your personal financial problems which will guide you successfully through a lifetime. This is a book you will not only want to read yourself, but will recommend to friends and give to young people just starting out in life. Free e-book: www.ccsales.com/the_richest_man_in_babylon.pdf

Secrets of the Millionaire Mind by T. Harv Eker. Learn how to identify and revise your own money blueprint to dramatically increase your income and accumulate wealth. This book appeared on the New York Times bestseller list and was #1 on the Wall Street Journal's business book list. Contact: www.secretsofthemillionairemind.com

Becoming Your Own Banker by R. Nelson Nash. This is an education on utilizing dividend-paying whole life insurance to put you on the path to financial independence and stop your nay-saying about life insurance. Contact: www.infinitebanking.org

Social Security Essentials by Dean Barber and Joe Elsasser. The authors bring your Social Security decisions into the real world and explores the interaction of various claiming options with the rest of your retirement financial life. Contact:

www.amazon.com/Social-Security-Essentials-Retirement-Income/dp/0989928411

Business/Entrepreneurship

Footprints of the Baker Boy by Henry F. Trione. By any measure, Henry Trione is one of Sonoma County's leading men of all time. His autobiography is not only about his upbringing and his extraordinary success and generosity, but also about opportunity, success and responsibility. Studying this book will give you clues for success and examples of what it means to be happy and secure in Sonoma County. Contact: www.trionebook.com

Be My Guest by Conrad Hilton. From proprietor of the Mobley Hotel in a dusty Texas oil town to the world's premier statesman of international hospitality, Conrad Hilton's spectacular rise helped rewrite the boundless opportunity of the American Dream. Here, in his own words, Conrad Hilton recounts the challenges and triumphs of a life brimming with adventure, celebrity, big business and unforgettable moments. In glamorous destinations across the globe, through more than seven decades of turbulence and prosperity, this is a thoroughly engaging saga. The world's best-known innkeeper lives up to the legend that helped bring the world closer together. An inspiring personal memoir that resonates with faith, perseverance, compassion and phenomenal success. Contact: www.amazon.com/Be-My-Guest-Conrad-Hilton/dp/B003RDU8OK

The E Myth by Michael Gerber. This book has led to a series of best-selling books. The author enlightens you as to why most small businesses don't work and what to do about it. If you're in business— read this book! Contact: www.amazon.com/The-Myth-Most-Businesses-About/dp/0887303625

General Success

How to Win Friends & Influence People by Dale Carnegie. One of the first best-selling self-help books ever published. First published in 1936, it has sold 15 million copies world-wide. Many successful and well known people cite Carnegie's book when discussing their path to success. Contact: www.dalecarnegie.com

Unlimited Power by Anthony Robbins. If you have ever dreamed of a better life, this perennial bestseller will show you how to achieve the extraordinary quality of life you desire and deserve. Anthony Robbins has proven to millions through his books, tapes and seminars that by harnessing the power of your mind you can do, have, achieve and create anything you want for your life. *Unlimited Power* is a revolutionary fitness book for the mind. It will show you, step by step, how to perform at your peak while gaining emotional and financial freedom, attaining leadership and self-confidence, and winning the cooperation of others. *Unlimited Power* is a guidebook to superior performance in an age of success. Contact: www.tonyrobbins.com

The Ultimate Success SECRET by Dan Kennedy. Is it possible that there is one single, super-powerful secret of success of far greater importance than all others? There is, and you can discover it hidden in this great little book. Contact: www.dankennedy.com

Create Your Own Future by Brian Tracy. An amazingly successful author, Tracy writes about his twelve critical factors of unlimited success for taking control of your life, your career, and your future. Contact: www.briantracy.com

* * * * *

The books listed above are ones I suggest you invest in for your library. Read them again and again. I believe you'll be richer for it.

Jim Rohn often said, *"Poor people have big TVs. Rich people have big libraries."* It sounds like a glib statement to be sure, since these days many rich people have big TVs too. The statement might offend you if you enjoy your TV, but that's not the point! The point is that successful people continually invest in developing their minds and creative pursuits, while unsuccessful people seem to seek instant self-gratification, which tends to default to doing stuff like watching junk on television.

Inspiration from one of my favorite books. . .

On February 11, 1919, he got his discharge from the Army at Camp Dix and took the first train for home. For three months after his return to Socorro, New Mexico, his life seemed completely without pattern or purpose. He was in fact restless, impatient, and depressed for the only time he could remember. He had come home from the war in France unscathed only to find he was a displaced person.

He considered possibilities all across America, then decided that he would go to Cisco, Texas (for the booming oil industry) and try to buy a bank. He had accumulated $5,011 and that is all he had when he got off the train in Cisco. He walked to the first bank he saw and began negotiating to buy it. That turned out to be a dead-end.

He needed some sleep so he went down the street to a two-story red brick building with the sign, "Mobley Hotel." There was a line out the door, and he saw a cash-cow of an opportunity . . . and ended up buying the hotel. After putting together the financing and taking title to the hotel, he went to the telegraph office and sent the following wire to his mom:

> "Frontier found. Water deep down here.
> Launched first ship in Cisco."

That night, with his hotel full up, he slept in the office and dreamed of a chain of Hilton hotels.

The life story of Conrad Hilton, *Be My Guest*, is one of my favorite books. It's a story of boom and bust, for a man and a nation. He says that the Great Depression tossed his life's work into a bottomless pit of debts, humiliations, and mortgages. But who remembers that now?

Conrad Hilton recounts his challenges and triumphs through more than seven decades of turbulence and prosperity. It's an inspiring personal memoir that resonates with faith, perseverance, compassion and phenomenal success.

This book would make an excellent gift for any young person graduating from high school or college. In addition, it would be an inspiring read for anyone feeling down or displaced. Conrad Hilton was one of the people you read about who came out of the Great Depression building and expanding his empire. We may be in a similar time in America's history, where financial devastation hits hard on the masses while certain others come out stronger and more financially secure.

America is a land of opportunity. I encourage you to find your frontier and launch your ship.

Other Irresistible Books by Montgomery Taylor

The New Rules of Success
(Celebrity Press, 2013)

Montgomery Taylor tells the story of how he grew up on a farm, worked for the FBI and then became a successful wealth advisor in a chapter entitled, "From Farm Boy to Wealth Manager." This is a compilation book—with 24 authors each being a Celebrity Expert® and illustrating their success with accomplishments that give them the authority and credibility to act as guide, tutor or mentor. When this book launched, it hit 7 best-seller lists on amazon!

Before It's Too Late— Retirement & Estate Solutions
(Bookstand Publishing, 2012)

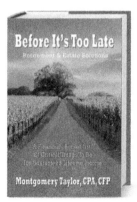

Regardless of whether you're retiring in the next decade or already retired, Taylor's well-researched financial strategies will have you rethinking your old retirement plan. With clear language and a wealth of fresh ideas, this book presents the financial "bucket list" of critical things to do for guaranteed lifetime income. No baby boomer should retire without checking this list—read this book and enjoy your best years while securing your financial future for yourself and your loved ones.

74 Tips to Eliminate College Cost Worries Almost Instantly
(College Plan Advisors, 2008)

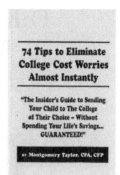

74 Tips to Eliminate College Cost Worries Almost Instantly

"The Insider's Guide to Sending Your Child to The College of Their Choice – Without Spending Your Life's Savings... GUARANTEED!"

BY Montgomery Taylor, CPA, CFP

Mr. Taylor discovered, after close to 30 years of working as a tax and financial advisor, that much of the information he had learned about financial planning for parents with college-bound children was actually wrong. This book sheds the light on bad advice provided and makes clear how to send your child to college without spending your life's savings.

Web Sites of Special Interest

www.taxwiseadvisor.com

Information about Montgomery Taylor's family of companies, services, books, free reports (i.e., *Planning Retirement Income; Tax Guide for Homeowners*), sign up for a complimentary newsletter and email tips.

www.taxwiseadvisor.com/blog/

Visit Monty's blog for an ongoing dialogue on financial topics aimed at informing you about methods of increasing your financial security.

www.ciorep.com

Information about free educational literature and seminar events for the public featuring top local professionals.

www.calethics.org

The California Ethics Foundation is a resource for business reporters and consumers on questions regarding ethics in financial service businesses.

http://montgomerytaylor.thenewrulesofsuccess.com

Information about *The New Rules of Success* book, free bonus chapter and more.

www.happyandsecureinsonomacounty.com

Information about this book and free resources linked to this book.

www.bookstandpublishing.com

Official site of Bookstand Publishing.

People Included in This Book

In this Resource Directory, you will find people mentioned in the book whom you might want to contact, listed in order of first appearance, by page number.

Patti Gribow   Page 22
The Patti Gribow Show
Phone: (760) 779-8800
Web: www.pgshow.com

Teresa Norton, Esq.   Page 28
Law Offices of Norton & Ingersoll, P.C.
Phone: (707) 230-2644
Web: www.noringlaw.com

Lawrence Lehr   Page 50
Allstate Insurance
Phone: (707) 546-3700
Web: www.agents.allstate.com/lawrence-lehr-santa-rosa-ca.html

Ronald Seaman   Page 85
Reverse Mortgage Consultant
Phone: (707) 544-6200
Email: ron@cypressfinancial.com

Kathleen Quinn   Page 92
Life Reflections Video
Phone: (707) 827-3208
Web: www.liferefectionsvideo.com

Larry Dahl   Page 94
Oil Stop
Phone: (707) 586-9934
Web: www.oilstopinc.com

Jeff Wandel   Page 94
Big O Tires
Fourth Street, Santa Rosa
Phone: (707) 528-2446

Mitch Silveira   Page 95
Silveira Buick GMC Dealership
Phone: (877) 891-4352
Web: www.silveiraautos.com

Tony Robbins   Page 97
Contact Taylor Weiss, Senior Peak Performance
Strategist
Phone: (424) 903-6107
Email: taylor.weiss@tonyrobbins.com

Tom Hopkins   Page 98
Phone: (800) 528-0446
Web: www.tomhopkins.com

Dan "Rudy" Ruettiger   Page 99
Phone: (800) 933-7839
Web: www.rudyintl.com

Jack Canfield   Page 109
Author, *Chicken Soup for the Soul*
Phone: (805) 563-2935
Web: www.jackcanfield.com

Dan Kennedy   Page 200
Glazer Kennedy Insiders Circle
Phone: (800) 871-0147
Web: www.gkic.com

Rocky Bleier   Page 224
Phone: (412) 621-2351
Web: www.rockybleier.com

Guest Experts

Rich Abazia   Page 111
Visit www.cypressfinancial.com to learn more about Rich and his
mortgage brokerage services. Or contact his Santa Rosa office at
(707) 544-6200.

Lucy Andrews, RN, MS   Page 121
Visit www.ayshomecare.net to learn more about Lucy and her
home care services. Or contact her Santa Rosa office at (707) 573-
1003, Larkspur office at (415) 461-6300.

Jeanne Browne, Esq.   Page 131
Visit www.jeannebrowne.com to learn more about Jeanne and her
family law services. Or contact her Santa Rosa office at (707) 575-
5162.

William F. Fritz, Esq.   Page 141
Visit www.fritzlawoffices.com to learn more about William and his
business legal services. Or contact his Santa Rosa office at (707)
578-8212.

Eric Gullotta, JD, CPA, MS (Tax)   Page 149
Visit www.gullottalaw.com to learn more about Eric and his estate
planning legal services. Or contact his Santa Rosa office at (707)
843-5257, Sonoma office at (707) 938-7234.

Kay Marquet   Page 159
Visit www.kaymarquet.com to learn more about Kay and her
philanthropic and consulting services. Or contact her Santa Rosa
office at (707) 527-0666.

Susan Pack   Page 169
Visit www.gilsonrealestate.com to learn more about Susan and her
real estate brokerage services. Or contact her Santa Rosa office at
(707) 484-5147 and susan@gilsonrealestate.com

Teri Sackett   Page 179

Visit www.sackettinsurance.net to learn more about Teri and her group health insurance services. Or contact her Sebastopol office at (707) 823-3689.

Business Client Directory

The following businesses are clients of Montgomery Taylor Family of Companies who requested they be included in this directory. I am enthusiastic about including their names here, but obviously cannot vouch for all of their products or services.

Matt Boothby
B&B Design
Drafting
Santa Rosa, CA
707-509-9747

Alanna Brogan, RN, MSN
Integrity Institute
5931 Monte Verde Drive
Santa Rosa, CA 95409
707-539-8000

Benjamin Bryant Construction
Fine Craftsmanship-Custom Home
Building-Remodeling
410 Grant Street
Healdsburg, CA 95448
707-535-9283

Robert Crase
Crase Trading and Investments
5829 Monte Verde Drive
Santa Rosa, CA 95409
707-573-6785

Michael Dennis
Project Controls and Forensics
448 South E Street
Suite 201
Santa Rosa, CA 95404
www.pcfconsultants.com
707-575-4652

Stephanie Endsley
Trinsic Animation
PO Box 494
Cazadero, CA 95421
www.trinsicanimation.com
855-337-6257

Jeff Erbst
Northbay Home Loans
1129 Industrial Avenue
Suite 102
Petaluma, CA 94952
www.NorthBayHomeLoans.com
707-246-7702

Dr. Thomas Fitzgerald, DPM
1041 Fourth Street
Santa Rosa, CA 95404
www.ThomasFitzgeraldDPM.com
707-568-1000

Susan Hagen
Author and Writing Guide
PO Box 443
Graton, CA 95444
www.Susanhagen.com
707-874-9223

Dr. Gordon Juriansz
Brookwood Internal Medical Association
500 Doyle Park Drive
Suite 304
Santa Rosa, CA 95405
707-545-1700

Jimmy James Page
Musician / Teacher
Petaluma, CA
www.jimmyjamespage.com
707-347-6997

Larry Pelton
Pelton Consulting Group
Fire & Explosion Investigations
PO Box 2826
Rohnert Park, CA 94927
www.Pcgfireinvestigations.vpweb.com
707-664-8111

Steven Raymond
Auto Spa
29653 Arnold Drive
Sonoma, CA 95476
www.auto-spa.com
707-938-8727

Janie Resing
Plain Jane's Consignments
18495 Sonoma Highway
Sonoma, CA 95476
www.plainjanesconsignments.com
707-939-7875

Denise Showalter
Jimmy Girl
Restyled Vintage Decor
12575 Los Amigos Road
Healdsburg, CA 95446
www.facebook.com/jimmygirlvintage
707-322-5565

Mark Wolocatiuk
The Driving Connection
Petaluma, CA 94954
www.thedrivingconnection.com
707-795-5369

Donna Yock, DMD
5300 Snyder Lane
Rohnert Park, CA 94928
www.donnayockdentist.com
707-586-1549

Johannes Zachbauer
Sonoma Coast Villa and Spa
16702 Shoreline Highway
Bodega, CA 94922
www.scvilla.com
707-876-7134

A Personal Afterword

In closing, I want to congratulate you on your commitment to learning and developing your potential. Thank you for allowing me to share my experiences and the tools that I use to manifest what I want in life.

Pretty much every year around Christmas, I watch the Christmas movie classic, *It's a Wonderful Life*. Maybe you've seen it many times as well and know the plot. George Bailey, played by Jimmy Stewart, grows up and dreams of travelling the world, but as it turns out he stays in Bedford Falls to manage the Bailey Building and Loan Association after his father passes away. The business has many ups and downs, but George hangs in there, always doing his best to be a good husband and father, and to make Bedford Falls a better place. But, as you know, things get ugly as he sees his youth, dreams and opportunities pass him by, and George attempts suicide. He is then given the opportunity to see what Bedford Falls would have been like without him. This is where we are able to see all the good he accomplished over the years and all the lives he positively impacted. The story is full of hope, tragedy, romance, and all the elements that make up real life.

Why am I closing by talking about *It's a Wonderful Life*? As you probably know, the movie is all about how we can all change the world for the better by making a positive impact. Well, you and I can both do that by building a happy and secure life for ourselves and our loved ones.

Life has been wonderful. God has blessed me. May He bless you too.

With my best wishes,

Monty

Montgomery Taylor

217

A Favor . . .

If you enjoyed Happy & Secure in Sonoma County, would you mind taking a minute to write a review on Amazon? Even a short review helps, and it would mean a lot to me.

On http://amazon.com, search for this book by title. Scroll down to the "Customer Reviews" section. Immediately to the right you'll see a button that says "Write a customer review." Click on that and write your own review. This actually works on any book, not just ones you've already purchased.

If people you care about may benefit from this book, please send them a copy. You might give one to them or merely provide them with a link to the book on Amazon, telling them how much you enjoyed it.

Better yet, call them up right now and arrange to meet them for coffee, and share this book with them. Lift them up! Be a mentor!

If you'd like to order copies of this book for your company, school, or group of friends, please go to:

www.happyandsecureinsonomacounty.com

. . . and a Request

We (the co-authors and I) have a request! We want you to write and tell us how this book has affected your life. Share your happy and secure stories with us. Let us know what you have done differently as a result of reading this book. What steps have you taken to secure your financial future? What new secrets have you learned about being happy and secure in Sonoma County? What tips do you have that we can pass on to future readers? Do you have a favorite story, quote or insight about being happy and secure that you would like to share with us? Please send it to us.

We are eager to hear from you. Thanks for contributing your story!

Please write to us at the following address:

Montgomery Taylor Family of Companies
2880 Cleveland Avenue, Suite 2
Santa Rosa, CA 95403
Or Email: Happy@taxwiseadvisor.com

Appendix 1

My Approach to Investing

The information I share here is based on my three decades in the investment industry, working through economic booms and busts, helping people achieve their financial objectives and always, always looking out for my clients' best interests.

Is Investment Return the Most Important Thing?

Well, if you're managing your own money or you've hired an "investment manager," I suppose the return on your investment is the most crucial element to measure. However, in the more holistic environment in which I operate, investment return is only one component. I charge a similar fee, about 1%, as other investment managers do, but I'm more of a "wealth manager" in the service I provide. Sure, I manage my clients' money, but I also advise them on taxes, insurance of all types, estate planning, retirement planning, college planning, divorce issues, buying and selling real estate, beneficiary designation issues and pretty much any aspect of financial life. What this really means is that for the 1% I'm being paid, I focus on helping my clients accomplish their dreams and financial objectives—not just trying to hit a stock market index performance number.

The Big Brokerage Firms are More Concerned with Their Risk than Yours...

Modern portfolio theory (MPT) aims to maximize investment returns by holding a mix of asset classes that move independently of each other through bull and bear market cycles. Economist Harry Markowitz introduced the concept in 1952 and won the 1990 Nobel Prize in economics. Big brokerage firms have followed this concept of investing ever since.

In my seven years working with the Sonoma County pension plan, I became very familiar with Modern Portfolio Theory and the strategic use of asset allocation as the means of diversification and reduction of risk. MPT is the practice among pension plans and large institutional money managers. It is taught in universities and has become the standard of practice by investment management firms and their financial advisors. They feel that they must adhere to the use of MPT for all clients and fear the potential liability repercussions if they do not.

Their concept (not mine) is to spread the invested money over many asset classes and stocks; some will go up, some will go down, most will stay relatively the same, and they will rebalance twice a year by selling some of the assets which have performed the best and buying some assets which have done poorly. MPT basically suggests that the market is efficient and all there is to know about any given stock or sector is already in the price. Therefore, there is nothing you can do to improve your odds of success. So stop trying.

No one realized until 2008 that all asset classes can go up or down at the same time. Oops, there went modern portfolio theory (MPT). It was discredited when investors lost money for the previous 10 year period. Here is what is confounding: MPT is still being pushed by brokerage firms simply because they have too much tied up in facilitating the failed strategy.

Brokers are taught MPT, as I was, even though it has been a losing strategy for decades now. I read an interview with the president of a brokerage firm about why they still push their advisors to use

MPT, and his answer was, *"We have spent too much money and invested too much infrastructure in this to stop now."*

Slowly but surely, investors are coming to realize there is another way and it isn't buy and hope. There is no question that real wealth can be made in the stock market, but this wealth can be wiped out just as quickly as it is made. There is an old market adage that goes like this: *"Bear markets return money to its rightful owners."*

This is why I run an independent firm, calling the shots and being free to adjust the allocations depending on what markets and sectors are in favor. I don't want some big corporate office telling me I have to follow MPT.

Seven Years of Pension Investment Experience

Having worked in the pension and institutional investment management arena, I see how it makes sense for pension plans to utilize MPT. It has to do with the fact that they have no time horizon. You and I, however, do have time horizons, life expectancies, retirement dates, and short term needs for money. So we shouldn't set our asset allocation and leave it to run on the rollercoaster of global stock markets. We need to be more dynamic.

The investment industry has evolved to support far better asset allocation solutions for the investor. I can deliver the benefits of strategic asset allocation and the dynamic adjustment of the allocation, through a portfolio of Exchange Traded Funds (ETFs), and do so in a way that addresses client suitability and the important market trends in force at any given time.

To be less reliant on MPT is to be more dynamic in allocating your investment dollars. In doing so, do we allocate more to stocks or to bonds or to some other asset class? Wonderful question! The answer is…it all depends on whether the market is on Offense or Defense.

Are Your Investments Playing Offense or Defense?

The chart below is a schematic of a football play like we often see on TV during football games. John Madden drew these diagrams on a monitor with his grease pencil showing what just happened on the last play. This chart is my way of demonstrating how you can view the stock market as a football game, where the play shifts from offense to defense throughout the game. A few football guys I know—Rocky Bleier (NFL 4 time Super Bowl Champion), Dan "Rudy" Ruettiger (inspiration for the film *Rudy*), and Leigh Steinberg (inspiration for the film *Jerry Maguire*)—would love this analogy. The first thing an investor must know before investing any money is whether the offensive team or the defensive team is on the field.

In a football game, two forces operate on the field at any one time: offense and defense. The same forces act in the marketplace. There are times when the market is supporting higher prices and times when the market is not supporting higher prices. When the market is 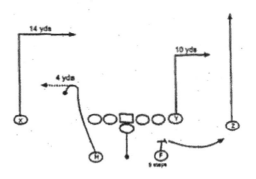 supporting higher prices, you have possession of the ball. You have the **offensive** team on the field. When you have the ball, your job is to take as much money away from the market as possible; this is when you must try to score. During times when the market is not supporting higher prices, you have in essence lost the ball and must put the **defensive** team on the field. During such periods, the market's job is to take as much money away from you as possible.

Think for a moment about your favorite football team. How well would they do this season if they operated with only the offensive team on the field every game? They might do well when they had possession of the ball, but when the opposing team had the ball, your team would be scored on at will. The net result is that your season would be lackluster at best. This is the problem most advisors have. They don't know where the game is being played, much less which team is on the field. I want to stress that there is a time to play offense and a time to play defense, and there are signals that indicate when the position of the ball is changing.

The football analogy comes from Thomas Dorsey in his book, *Point and Figure Charting*, which I've been studying. The concept has been numerically quantified by several studies, including one by the University of Chicago and another described by Benjamin F. King in his book, *The Latent Statistical Structure of Securities Price Changes* (Chicago: University of Chicago Press, 1964).

"Tilting" Your Investments to Offense or Defense

Once you're aware of the real condition of the market, you'll know which asset classes to add money to or take money from. You can think of this as a tactical maneuver to overweight or "tilt" your portfolio allocation towards those asset classes which are out-performing and away from those which are underperforming.

> You can learn more about this approach to investing by reading Thomas Dorsey's book or by following the instructions in the Resources section of this book to request a free report I wrote titled *Better Retirement Returns!—For Better Returns Than CalPERS—Last 10 Years*.

Appendix 2

The Peace of Mind Retirement Planning Pyramid

I've taken the pyramid concept and applied it to the complete retirement and estate planning process. Each building block of the pyramid represents an important financial component in your overall financial plan. I'm sure you can imagine how weak and flawed the pyramid would be if it were missing a number of the blocks. It just isn't likely to withstand the test of time and would one day crumble if there were holes left in it. No engineer would do such a thing.

And yet, isn't that exactly what happens when your advisors are only skilled in one block of your financial pyramid? Your tax guy does his thing. Your attorney does her thing. Your investment guy is doing his thing and your insurance people are doing their thing. Sure, they may all be great at what they do. The question is though, is each advisor's work fashioned in such a way that it integrates perfectly with every other component of your financial life? Does it effectively and efficiently accomplish your lifetime financial objectives and allow you to be worry free, at least financially?

The planning pyramid I've designed and illustrated below includes each of the components I wrote about in my previous book, *Before It's Too Late: Retirement & Estate Solutions*. Each block solves some potential problem in your financial life, with the intention of giving you an integrated, comprehensive plan for your retirement and your estate. But most importantly, this level of holistic planning should provide you with peace of mind, comfort and certainty. In our uncertain times, we can all benefit from some certainty with regard to our money.

This pyramid is the subject of my previous book, *Before It's Too Late: Retirement & Estate Solutions.*

FREE OFFERS AND RESOURCES FROM MONTGOMERY TAYLOR

Free Stuff Linked to this Book

To help you get full value from this book, there is a collection of

FREE EXTRA RESOURCES

waiting for you at

www.happyandsecureinsonomacounty.com

- FREE: Net Worth Planning Statement, Excel Spreadsheet
- FREE: 57 Point Financial Health Checklist
- FREE: The Five Great Goals of Life & Where Are You Today? Worksheets
- FREE: Social Security Optimization Report
- FREE: "Tax Bomb" White Paper
- FREE: Better Retirement Returns Report

. . . and every other extra resource referred to throughout this book.

Bring the Power of *Happy & Secure in Sonoma County* to Your Organization:

The Happy & Secure Workshop

Positive and profound changes will be the result when your employees, managers, members, and students experience *The Happy & Secure Workshop*.

Not only will your team be inspired and motivated to achieve greater success, but they'll also learn how to balance life's demands while building a strong financial foundation.

The Happy & Secure Workshop will benefit employers or other organizations. Providing financial education for employees often results in improvements in financial wellness and performance ratings, and reductions in absenteeism, turnover, health care costs, and workplace distractions.

Companies offering 401(k) retirement plans can be provided with customized asset allocation reports for their employees. These reports break down the investment choices by asset class and also provide a proprietary relative strength ranking. This provides meaning and guidance to employees managing their 401(k) retirement fund.

The Happy & Secure Workshop includes financial tools and highly customized program materials for each participant. Single session or multiple session workshop formats can be designed for your organization. *The Happy & Secure Workshop* is ideal for groups such as:

- Hospital and medical office personnel
- Managers and executives
- Trade association memberships
- Corporate workgroups, new hires, pre-retirees
- Students and educators
- School business officials and administrators
- Professional practitioners and their staffs

232

For more information, please contact us:

Montgomery Taylor Family of Companies
2880 Cleveland Avenue, Suite 2, Santa Rosa, CA 95403
Phone (707) 576-8700
Email: <u>Workshop@taxwiseadvisor.com</u>

About Monty

A Quilly Award winning Best-Selling Author, Montgomery Taylor, CPA, CFP is known as one of the top wealth managers for high net-worth individuals in the United States. His role has been helping them have peace of mind with a sound road map for achieving their financial objectives. His firm passed the rigorous testing of the National Association of Board Certified Advisory Practices (NABCAP) and made their prestigious list of top wealth managers. His book, *The New Rules of Success,* has been used as a textbook on achieving life success for university students.

The CEO of the Montgomery Taylor Family of Companies, a multi-disciplinary financial services firm with more than 400 clients in 16 states, Monty was recognized as one of the top thought leaders in the business world and selected as a speaker by the National Academy of Best-Selling Authors. His unique perspective on solving financial uncertainties has led him to develop a client service method he calls Wealth Integration Review, helping to assure his clients that they will never have to worry about running out of money.

Monty has appeared as a speaker on programs with Tom Hopkins (business success expert), Jack Canfield (*Chicken Soup For The Soul*), Leigh Steinberg (inspiration for the film *Jerry Maguire*), Dan "Rudy" Ruettiger (inspiration for the film *Rudy*), Patti Gribow (*Leading Experts* TV show host), Nick Nanton (Emmy Award winning director) Dan Kennedy (business author and speaker), and Rocky Bleier (NFL 4 time Super Bowl Champion). In addition, Monty has spoken to many church groups and company employee groups.

Monty has been seen in *USA Today, The Press Democrat, NorthBay BIZ* magazine and the *North Bay Business Journal.* He has appeared on E!, a satellite television channel owned by NBC, The Patti Gribow Show airing on the Comcast Hometown Network, and on radio stations KZST, KJZY and KTRY, speaking on financial subjects from his books *Before It's Too Late—Retirement & Estate Solutions* and *New Rules of Success.* Monty is a member of the Leadership

Circle at KRCB Public Television Channel 22 and a Columnist for the *North Bay Business Journal*.

Monty grew up in the beautiful wine country of the Alexander Valley, where his family was one of the founding owners of Chateau Souverain Winery. He now lives in Santa Rosa with his wife, Terri. Their two daughters and one son live in Colorado. Monty enjoys the beach, outdoor activities, traveling with his family, and attending local theater. He is active in many community and professional organizations, and is a past President of the Redwood Empire Estate Planning Council.

Currently Monty spends his time writing, teaching and managing financial matters for his clients. He takes on a limited number of new clients each year. Inquiries about becoming a client should be directed to the offices of Montgomery Taylor at (707) 576-8700.

Mr. Taylor is available for speaking engagements, schedule permitting. Call to inquire. Information about his popular Tax & Investment Newsletter as well as his other books is available at www.TaxWiseAdvisor.com.